# HELIGAN

## A PORTRAIT OF THE LOST GARDENS

# HELIGAN

## A PORTRAIT OF THE LOST GARDENS

TOM PETHERICK

*photography by*

MELANIE ECLARE

WEIDENFELD & NICOLSON

# Contents

# Foreword

The moment I saw Tom I had a feeling about him. What began as a short conversation seamlessly turned into a dialogue on a variety of enthusiasms ranging from coffee growing to race horses, from Permaculture to the economy of Cornwall. With his easy grin and views far to the left of those suggested by first impressions of his accent or background, Tom was a delight.

His love of the countryside and those that work it made him ideal for the adventures that lay ahead, and that is how a casual request for a few months' work in between careers turned into a life-changing event.

As our Sleeping Beauty shrugged off its blanket of decay and emerged blinking into the sunshine and into the hearts of our many visitors, it was Tom who led the wild bunch that tamed the land and made the productive gardens burst with life once more.

It should be a distant memory, but every year I am reminded of it as the rows of vegetables, soft fruit and cut flowers take up station once again – Peter Rabbit for grown ups! I am reminded of it when I see the wall fruit ripening, the cucumbers, melons and strawberries tempting me. I am reminded of it when I eat a white-fleshed peach from the Peach House or taste the sweet grapes from the Vineries. I smile wistfully in the Potting Shed at flowers in vases, raffia and terracotta – good and wholesome – but most of all I am reminded of it when I see the pineapples; Jamaica Queen and Cayenne, oh how exotic their names and their past. I remember that moment of pure joy as we all stood around the Pineapple Pit and marvelled at the first blush of fruit. It brought the gardens to a standstill. We didn't care that it was the most expensively produced pineapple in history, it was ours – we had grown it successfully for the first time in more than a hundred years. Now at last we were the true heirs to those that had made these gardens great.

Thank you Tom for the privilege of having you there and the pleasure it has given me and everyone else. Thank you Melanie for capturing in pictures the spirit of a place that changed not only my life, but many others, and which I hope will continue to do so long into the future.

RIGHT *This map shows the gardens as they are today. The Northern Gardens, which include the productive gardens, are situated behind, or to the north of, Heligan House. The Jungle runs due south of the house and into the Lost Valley, which winds its way to the north-east.*

# Heligan

*Key areas of the garden are numbered. Whilst it may seem curious that the ornamental and productive gardens are sited behind the house, it should be emphasised that the land falls away steeply below the house to the Jungle and the Lost Valley.*

1   Flora's Green

2   Northern Summerhouse

3   Vegetable Garden

4   Ravine

5   Western Shelterbelt

6   Italian Garden

7   Melon Yard

8   New Zealand

9   Horsemoor Hide

10  Flower Garden

11  Sundial Garden

12  Lost Valley

13  Jungle

# Introduction

I always knew Heligan was there. It was stuck somewhere in my subconscious. Perhaps it came from childhood trips to Hemmick Beach, which lies to the west of the Dodman Point on the Roseland Peninsula, only four or five miles from the gardens. We would pass the entrance to the drive on our way to pick mussels and swim in the summer. Heligan would come up in conversation, fleetingly, as though it warranted a mention but not much more: 'Poor Heligan, I wonder what will ever become of it?'

But from afar the trees were always visible. Tall Monterey pines guarding the entrance to something exciting that had once been treasured and needed protection, as the Montereys were planted to do. They were visible from Pentewan Hill to the east and from almost as far as Truro to the west. There was a feeling of forbidden fruit about the place, that it wasn't to be touched. Had Heligan been in cycling distance (it is the hills not the distance that matter in Cornwall) then it would have been on my list to explore, but I never made it then. I had to wait, but it was worth it.

ABOVE *My grandfather, Gerald Petherick, in the uniform of a lieutenant in the Devon Yeomanry, on the deck of the SS* Olympic *which transported the regiment to Suvla Bay in 1915. The photograph is believed to have been taken by the ship's captain.*

## The Heligan Connection

In the spring of 1915 my grandfather, George Gerald Petherick of Porthpean House near St Austell in Cornwall, boarded the SS *Olympic* as a lieutenant in the Devon Yeomanry and sailed for Suvla Bay and the Gallipoli Campaign in the First World War. The fighting dragged on until the winter and became one of the most infamous of that dreadful war, for its huge loss of life (a total of over half a million on both sides), the extreme, even suicidal bravery of the combatants and the stubbornness of the allied commanders – including Winston Churchill, who was fortunate to salvage his political reputation. On evacuation back to England my grandfather, suffering from the traumatic events of war, was sent to Heligan House; only five miles from Porthpean, it was the home of his neighbours the Tremaynes, who had lent it to the nation as a convalescent home for the wounded.

There are pictures in my grandmother's photograph books of 'GGP' strolling through new plantings of large-leaved rhododendrons in the garden around the house, or leaning against huge tree ferns in the valley that even then had attained substantial size. Seventy-six years on from Gallipoli I began work in that same garden, which now lay under a heavy blanket of bramble, having descended into obscurity as one by one the gardening staff failed to return from the Great War. Unlike my grandfather I had no war to recover from, but stepping into that garden opened up a chapter in my life which has profoundly affected me.

The restoration that has become known simply as 'The Lost Gardens of Heligan', and here I should point out that for pronunciation purposes the emphasis is on the second syllable of the word Heligan, has captured the imagination of well over a million visitors since it opened in 1991. This wonderful garden and its adjoining estate have literally been brought back from the dead. During the period from the end of the First World War until the restoration project got under way, most of the garden fell into disrepair. After seventy-five years the level of decay was pitiful and unchecked growth was impassable in many places. Abundant rainfall through the warm Cornish winters had submerged the garden under a shroud of moss and lichen, and gently put it to sleep.

In 1990 Tim Smit and John Nelson, the two men behind the project, fought their way through bramble and nettle and into the dark recesses of the gardens; as they did so they began to uncover a nineteenth-century horticultural diamond which they knew they had to salvage. Twelve years of restoration have passed in which so much has been learned, achieved and enjoyed, I live in hope that those who created this beautiful garden, through the nineteenth century and before, look kindly on our endeavours.

## The Beginnings of the Project

As a child my summers were spent at Porthpean, where long days were passed sailing, swimming, shrimping and lazing on the beach. Only a mile and a half from St Austell, Porthpean has always served as the 'town beach'. It is lively in the summer with the shrieks of children running in and out of the sea, dogs barking and the tinkling anthem of Mrs Kelly's ice cream van. It faces east over the clear expanse of St Austell Bay to the Gribbin Head, behind which nestles the port of Fowey. From there the china clay, which is still mined in the hills behind St Austell, is shipped all over the world. It was an idyllic place to spend the summer.

My grandfather died in 1946. The house in which he lived, and in which my father spent many childhood summers, passed to his eldest son David, who immediately sold it back to his two uncles, my grandfather's brothers. Retired from politics and the army respectively, they kept up a good garden and it was within the walls at Porthpean that my early horticultural instincts were stirred. The head gardener was a tall figure called Pope. Kindly but authoritative, he wore a trilby hat, waistcoat, shirt and tie, stout shoes and a white apron, two clean ones per week. He lived in Ivy Cottage opposite the church in Porthpean village and oversaw the garden and the work. To my untrained, boyish eye he appeared to confine himself to the nice jobs like pollinating the peaches in the peach houses and thinning grapes in the vinery, but in reality he was a proper old-fashioned head gardener. He delivered the vegetables to Effy the cook and cut the camellias for the Cornwall Garden Society Spring Flower Show. The real work was done by his two under-gardeners, one of whom, Tony Tregilgas, has been at Porthpean for fifty years and is now my parents' head gardener. The walled gardens at Porthpean held unearthly

BELOW *My grandfather and his dog Spot standing underneath a tree fern (Dicksonia antarctica) in the Jungle. It is hard to pinpoint the location but it may be around the third pond. The plant's foliage is particularly abundant and its girth is enormous, much bigger than any seen in the garden today.*

pleasures for me: a stolen peach, a ripening tomato, and definitely unripe apples (what apple is ever ripe on the tree for a young boy?). Those early forays into the world of horticulture did not become an obsession because the beach and its delights were paramount then; but the seeds of my interest were sown, and to this day I have retained a fascination for walled gardens and all the things edible and inedible that grow within them.

With my horticultural training behind me, I had not long returned from another trip – to Tamil Nadu in South India, where I had been helping regenerate a redundant coffee and fruit farm – when I heard that something was going on at Heligan. Quite what was actually happening was not clear, so I went along with a friend and paid to get in. We had barely crossed the drive and passed beneath the tunnel of tangled laurel when the sensation hit us. By the time we had walked down through the beginnings of a Vegetable Garden and reached the Melon Yard, which was half jungle, half building site, I knew I was going to work there. The feeling was one of raw excitement. It was like the first day of spring – the energy in the garden was so incredibly alive, it was magnetic. Just as all visitors did, we slid around in the mud and lurched through the tangled mess in the Jungle, bumping against huge tree ferns and treading over the dry, crackling leaves of that season's dying gunnera foliage. The spiky plumes of exotics such as *Cordyline australis* were battling against the encroaching tide of sycamores, and everywhere there were trees desperate to be freed from this choking mass.

That there is a sense of romance about a walled garden is a given for me, but even during those first few hours it was plain that this project was special; it was precisely the right thing for Heligan, and the garden knew that and was opening itself up. The atmosphere was thick with emotion. The place was bursting with joy, perhaps at being released from years of sorrowful neglect, and it definitely needed me. We got home in a state of high excitement, and so determined was I to get involved that I rang up the man in charge, Tim Smit, that very night. The next day I found myself back there, sitting in a cabin filled with slim panatella smoke, telling him just how much he needed me. To my delight he hired me on the spot, beginning a long association between myself and Heligan, that most extraordinary of gardens.

ABOVE *As the woodlands and shelterbelts throughout Heligan have been cleared of years of debris, the light has found its way back in to the garden once again. Bluebells and primroses now burst forth in early spring and bring to life the woodland floor.*

The timing was perfect. Much of the clearing of what has become known as the Northern Gardens had been done by the time I started work in the autumn of 1993. The layers of leaf mould that had encased the paths had been rolled back like carpets, revealing the original network almost completely intact. Vigorous growth of volunteer species (that is, prolific, diligent self-seeders such as sycamore) was everywhere, but almost, it seemed, as a protective mechanism to shelter the treasures that lay beneath. Just as the top few inches of a compost heap create a hard skin to protect the industry taking place beneath, so had the garden created its own skin.

The dormant period of winter is the best time to ease your way into a garden, to try to come to terms with it and allow it to get used to you. As the garden and its plants begin to move into hibernation, the time is right for a new person to become involved with it. The moment had arrived to reverse the process of seventy-five years of decay, and what better place to begin than in the most enormous Vegetable Garden imaginable. Everything was

perfect: a gentle southerly slope, impeccable topsoil at least eighteen inches deep with barely a stone in it (they had all been cleaned off by young apprentice gardeners many years before), and good shelter on all sides, yet very little shade. I was quivering with delight and my mind was working overtime. Soil nutrition would have to be attended to — so many years of weeds with no nutrition except leaf fall and the manure from small mammals and birds is not enough to nourish soil. It is good for building soil life and keeping it in good health, but insufficient for high levels of cropping.

Being thrown into this maelstrom of activity was energising. There was an extraordinary mix of people playing a number of very diverse roles: volunteers, builders, conservationists, garden historians and gardeners. By that time the restoration was in full swing, rocketing along with a kind of boundless energy where inspiration, talent and ideas were always encouraged. In the front rank of this eclectic bunch of enthusiasts three men stood head and shoulders above the rest. Tim Smit, the affable ideas man and founder of the project, who is now found mainly at his other brainchild the Eden Project a few miles away; John Nelson, his business partner and co-founder, the builder and the grafter; and Philip McMillan Browse, the horticulturist, ex-head of RHS Wisley and the man who provided the plant knowledge. Somehow those three managed to instil the right mix of self-belief, sense of humour and frenetic work ethic to drive the project forward. Tim roared around the garden, the county and the world telling anyone who would listen about what we were doing. He was a massive inspiration and a pure joy to be around. His foil, John Nelson, had the eye to restore old buildings and old dreams that was essential to the project. John led from the front and I have never seen a man work so hard and give so much of himself to a place. His passion was all-consuming; whether it was laying cobbles or draining ditches John was there, day in, day out, getting the job done and earning maximum respect from the troops. Philip approached the horticultural side of things with thorough professionalism. The research he put into reassembling the walled gardens and the Vegetable Garden in particular was painstaking. There are now few bodies left from those early days. John's friend Dave Burns is in charge of the car park and Charles Fleming is still doing exactly what he was the day I arrived — weeding in the Vegetable Garden. Philip is also still in place as horticultural director, having

TOP *Heligan House at the beginning of the twentieth century. The creeper could be ivy or Virginia creeper, it is hard to tell. It no longer remains and the brick house, finished c.1690, is now painted an off-white colour.* LEFT *An early photograph of the Paxtonian Vinery in the Flower Garden before anyone laid a hand on it. All the glasshouses in the garden had reached a pitiful level of decay and had to be torn down and rebuilt in their entirety.*

PREVIOUS PAGE *The Jungle in midsummer. The* Gunnera manicata *in the foreground is nearly ten feet high, extraordinary for a herbaceous plant. The yellow bracts of* Cornus capitata *are visible to the left under the pompon of the chusan palm,* Trachycarpus fortunei. *The central splash of pink is rosebay willowherb,* Epilobium angustifolium.

spent much of the last few years helping to put the Eden Project together. And I am there, although I was absent between 1997 and 2001, during which time I was growing organic fruit and vegetables from two redundant walled gardens in Dorset.

We all put in enormous effort, but there were always rumours of terrible financial hardships – both John and Tim had mortgaged their houses, we were led to believe – and there were scant funds, other than those coming in from the visitors. There were a few volunteers in the garden and those of us who were paid felt lucky. How we survived is a miracle, how anything ever got paid for is a mystery; every time I walk through the rhubarb patch I smile to think that had Philip not reached for his credit card, the Scottish nurseryman who supplied the plants would never have parted with them. As we set to work on Philip's plan for the Vegetable Garden amidst the chaos and the magic, we did so without really knowing whether or not we would get paid at the end of the week. Somehow, though, it didn't matter; it was fun and it was absolutely sure to be a success, of that there was an underlying feeling of certainty. There was a strong sense that something about the garden was driving us forward – provided we showed the right amount of respect for this magnificent place, its past, and all the years of love, devotion, knowledge and skill that had been poured into it.

This curious mixture of decay and resurgence, so fundamental to the project at that time, pushed us on into the deepest interior of a garden that had once been great, and whose hour had come again. The plan that Tim, John and Philip had settled into by 1993 was to make the productive gardens the centrepiece of the restoration, around which everything else would fit into place. The restoration of such a range of derelict glasshouses as there were, lying bruised and battered throughout the walled gardens, would save the soul of this neglected treasure. At the top of the list was the ruined, ivy-clad Pineapple Pit. What a find: a giant frame given over entirely to the production of fresh pineapples; it was in itself a giant monument to what was increasingly appearing to be a state of the art Victorian kitchen garden. There is something extraordinarily romantic about these areas behind the walls. At times you can reach out and touch the history; a glance at a rusted old tool head, or a rack of cobwebbed terracotta pots, can transport you right back to the times when men in hob-nailed boots pushed wooden wheelbarrows filled with steaming horse manure in these very gardens.

The spring of 1994 saw us getting underway with the plan that Philip had worked out for the Vegetable Garden. With that, after much agonising, came the removal of the last remaining apple tree in that garden, to great dismay from public and pundits alike. It was a seminal moment, a statement of intent which said that in order to be professional, sacrifices must be made. This is still one of the biggest issues that we face today; woe betide the gardener who puts progress to the fore without careful thought. There is a belief that we must show the old side of Heligan whilst at the same time bringing in the best of the new. The restoration and the garden today would be nothing without the garden that was the past, whether mid nineteenth-century or mid twentieth-century decay.

To our amazement and quiet relief, the weather during that summer of 1994 brought in visitors. We knew we had something to show them; for many of us, Heligan had never gone

LEFT *John Nelson, one of the co-founders of the project, removes ivy from a tree fern at the start of the restoration to allow the new growth through. In winter onion sacks are filled with leaves and placed on the crown of the plant, to prevent the frost from getting in and killing it. The plants are more likely to encounter frost in the Northern Gardens than in the Jungle.*

away, it had simply gone to sleep and needed to be gently nudged awake. However we did not anticipate that the garden would be overrun with visitors in the space of two years. In those days, or back along, as they say in Cornwall, the awestruck visitor was a common sight. Perhaps this is why, to this day, all the older staff and many of the young still enjoy talking to visitors and spinning a few yarns. That was all part of the fun. And it has always been part of the day's work. In turn, the visitors come away informed, educated and entertained. We are all gardeners when visiting other gardens, and comments such as 'your leeks are a bit behind' or 'we could do with a drop of rain' are excuses to instigate far-reaching conversations about allotments in Burnley or grandmothers who were in service in large households up and down the country many years ago. The visitors are our lifeblood because the garden depends entirely upon them. They treat the garden with the respect it deserves and it is a joy to see so many people enjoying themselves, even if there is not much room to move after opening time on a July morning. They stand and stare and comment on our dedication to the job, how our backs must ache and how we can come and help in their gardens when we have finished in our own. They never complain if we push past in a hurry and they are unstinting in their praise.

And with those visitors came journalists, garden writers, photographers and all the others attracted by the buzz associated with the beginnings of an exciting new project. It very quickly became evident that Heligan was going to create news in the gardening world. This meant, however, that we would have to look to our laurels and work to maintain the highest possible standards. It was an extraordinary year because the pace of everything that was going on was so extreme; and by the end of that year it began to dawn on us that so much of the restoration that we had hoped and planned for might become a reality.

Ornamental Heligan | Productive Heligan | Wild Heligan

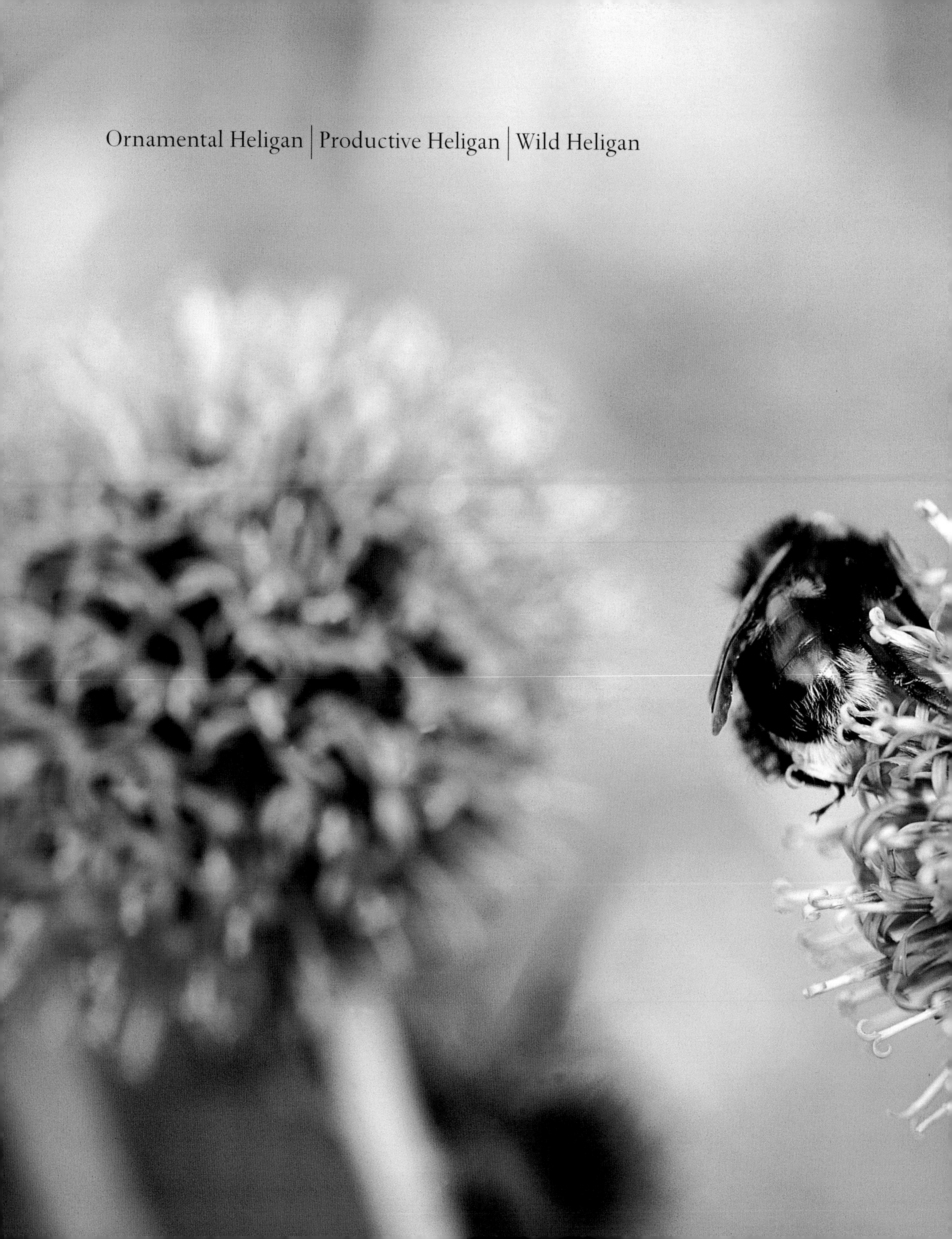

# 1 Flora

*The passion and energy that Henry Hawkins Tremayne injected into his estate was the turning point in its development. It laid the foundations for the bonanza of horticulture that filled gardens like Heligan with plants that had never been seen before.*

# *Ornamental*
# Heligan

LEFT *Early morning light filters through the woodland canopy of the Jungle and on to the majestic tree ferns. The crinkly-leaved fern in the right foreground is* Blechnum chilense, *which is to be found throughout the garden.* ABOVE *An unnamed* Camellia japonica. *Heligan is not strongly represented by camellias, which is a shame considering the large collection of rhododendrons which came from Sir Joseph Hooker's exploits abroad. It appears that someone in the garden's history did not have a passion for them.*

For me the excitement has always begun with the climb from sea level up the curves of Pentewan Hill, a mile and a half short of the garden. From Tregiskey Cross, at the top of the hill, the last remaining Monterey pines and the two big oaks to the east of the Vegetable Garden are visible as the right turn is made. From Peruppa Farm, over the bridge that clears the old drive, still lined with thick banks of *Rhododendron ponticum*, you turn the corner and there is the entrance to Heligan, guarded by a thick grove of holm oaks (*Quercus ilex*).

## What Went There Before Us

Heligan is a large but narrow garden. It spans some seventy acres and is divided into two quite distinct areas, the Northern Gardens, which comprise the pleasure grounds and productive gardens, and to the south a valley garden known as the Jungle. This adjoins another valley known as the Lost Valley and together the two have become the Southern Gardens. Bisecting the Northern and Southern Gardens lies Heligan House, a fine William and Mary mansion which probably reached completion around 1690. It is built out of brick, which is very unusual for Cornwall, where granite conquers all. Now split up into flats and entirely separate from the restoration project, it was sold to Heligan House Ltd in 1970.

The history of the garden goes back through generations to the end of the seventeenth century, when the house was built and gardens laid out around it. Although there have been

Tremaynes at Heligan since 1569, it was not until the Reverend Henry Hawkins Tremayne took the helm in 1766 on the death of his elder brother that the garden began to enter a more serious phase. By the end of the eighteenth century the walled gardens had been built and the rides down which we walk today were in place on either side. Heligan and the Tremaynes, who lived in it until just after the Second World War, offer a typical example of what life was like among the squirearchy throughout the eighteenth, nineteenth and first half of the twentieth centuries. At the highest, northernmost point of the garden there is a huge lawn surrounded by skirts of 150-year-old rhododendrons. If you imagine a body running from top to bottom, the lawn would be the face, the rhododendrons the hair, the Vegetable Garden the heart and lungs, the eastern and western rides that run down the sides of the garden the arms and the Jungle, or valley garden, the long legs running down to the sea at Mevagissey. The passion and energy that Henry Hawkins Tremayne injected into his estate was the turning point. It laid the foundations for the bonanza of horticulture that filled Heligan, and other nineteenth-century gardens like it, with plants that had never been seen before.

There are key moments in horticulture, and the first trip made by Sir Joseph Hooker to India was definitely one of them. That expedition by the second director of the Royal Botanical Gardens at Kew, undertaken from 1848 through to 1850, yielded some spectacular results. His findings in Sikkim, which was then its own kingdom but is now in the north-easternmost reaches of India where the Himalayas peter out and meet China, are still in evidence at Heligan. Flora's Green, as this huge lawn at the top of the pleasure grounds is known, is ringed by giant Cornish Red rhododendrons. Their growth fuses together to make an impenetrable wall of huge, round boulders 20 feet high. They flower profusely in April, producing a mass of very dark pink to red blooms around which bees swarm in their thousands, drunk on their nectar. Nobody has touched these enormous plants for a century and a half, and their dense interiors are home to a wealth of birds and mammals, including tree creepers and nuthatches, which migrate between these and the last of the big oaks that are dotted around the garden. There are also rabbits living in these rhododendrons, a little too close to the Vegetable Garden for comfort. Two seasons ago a rogue rabbit jumped the chicken wire fence that surrounds it and took up residence, causing mayhem among the rows of carrots. After a walk through all the crops failed to reveal his whereabouts, I began to sweat. After another night's grazing put paid to a row of young parsnips, panic took a hold. It takes experience and a deft touch to hoe rows of onions 100 feet long when there are only 18 inches between the rows and 6 inches between the plants; but our tractor man Mike Rundle grew up hoeing whole fields of turnips at Ardevereaux near Tresilian, one of Cornwall's most beautiful farms, and it is to him that we look when the onions need a hoe through them. And that was where Mike found that our furry friend had scraped himself a hole: right in the middle of the onion patch. He found the scrape but we never found the rabbit; he knew his time had come so he moved on.

The big Cornish Red rhododendrons are seen in many of the great gardens of Cornwall, such as Trebah on the Helford River and Tregrehan near Par, and have become a signature

plant for Cornwall. The big sweep of them up behind the house at Chyverton, near Truro, is particularly impressive. Hooker's rhododendron collection is well represented at Heligan, and numbers among it various different species including *Rhododendron thomsonii, R. falconeri* and *R. griffithianum*. This widespread collecting of rhododendrons in the late nineteenth century instigated a kind of 'rhododendromania', which swept through the gardens of the upper classes and those with new money, especially in Cornwall where soil and climate were quickly shown to be suitable. Close neighbours and relations of the Tremaynes, the Rashleighs of Menabilly, near Par, planted two acres of rhododendrons, calling the area 'Hooker's Grove'. One of the many miracles of Heligan – and perhaps the biggest driving force behind the restoration – is just how it was that so many great and ancient plants survived the years of fallen trees and general decay. The ring of rhododendrons around Flora's Green has remained completely intact. There is a perfect specimen of *R. niveum* tucked away in the north-west corner, which grows quite happily, producing its incomparable tight mauve heads each year in May. There are also a number of very impressive specimens of a large-leaved species of rhododendron called *R. falconeri* (which Hooker named after his friend Hugh Falconer, Superintendent of the Calcutta Botanic Gardens) dotted throughout the garden. This plant has enormous cream flowers to complement its huge leaves, which regularly reach two feet

in length. For the garden visitor hoping to see some spring colour this first sight of Flora's Green on a sunny April morning is quite spectacular: a lawn the size of a football pitch, surrounded on three sides by a wall of brilliant red. It could be too much, too overwhelming, yet by some quirk of nature each bloom of the Cornish Red is slightly different in shade. This, I think, softens the blow. It is an awesome sight. By July, when the rhododendrons are well and truly over and red flower has been replaced by green leaf, another signature plant of Heligan comes into flower. Tucked away in a forgotten nook at the back of Flora's Green is the oldest surviving specimen of *Cornus capitata*. One of the least seen of the *Cornus* family, this modest tree once lined the entire drive from Heligan House to the road that runs between Pentewan and St Austell, a distance of at least two miles. It has pretty butter-yellow bracts which are followed by red seed pods that look like lychees. Their yellow flesh is tasty when very ripe, but you have to beat the squirrels and the blackbirds to them (and be sure to spit out the seeds when you are done). Considering that Flora's Green was allegedly used as a tank park by the US army during the Second World War, it is even more surprising that the great plants have survived. To accommodate the machines of war a layer of concrete was laid down (the lime content of which could not have been helpful), which then had to be broken up and removed in 1992 before the garden opened to make way for the lawn to be reseeded.

Two other lucky survivors from the mid nineteenth century, which lie around Flora's Green are a giant *Magnolia campbellii* (another Hooker introduction, named after Dr Archibald Campbell, the political agent to Sikkim) and a Douglas fir (*Pseudotsuga menziesii*), which has a pronounced dwarfing gene. The magnolia is very large and ancient with flowers that are darker than many other *M. campbellii* seedlings. This huge tree, well over thirty feet high, goes on and on, flowering year after year, and every season a north-westerly wind comes along and plays havoc with it. It is sited at the back of Flora's Green at the highest point of the garden. For its topmost blooms there is no shelter from the ravages of the pounding westerly. If you were to stand in the car park on the north-western shoulder of the estate and look west, there is not much above you on the skyline. You can see as far as the wind turbines at St Newlyn East and on a sunny day, with the right eyes, all the way to the Atlantic Ocean at the north coast. It is no good asking the south coast of Ireland to intervene on our behalf to break the wind; there is only ocean between us and America, so if it blows with intent from the west there is nothing in the way to stop it. The poor magnolia catches plenty of this punishment. Yet there is no more beautiful sight than those pink blooms, each the size of a small football, against a dark, storm-laden sky on a bright spring day. Although magnolias were in cultivation in England by the late seventeenth century, Hooker must have been particularly pleased with his find, describing it as 'an immense...sparingly branched tree, leafless during the winter and also during the flowering season, when it puts forth...great rose-purple cup-shaped flowers.' By far the tallest tree in the garden, its topmost branches are utterly exposed. Its plight highlights the desperate need for shelter in Cornish gardens, even more so at altitude. Five hundred feet above sea level is very high for a garden as close to the sea as Heligan, and this is why it is ringed by distinct shelterbelts on three sides: north, east and west. Cherry laurel was mainly

ABOVE *Jimmy Lee. Whilst there is no reference to a J. Lee as a member of the gardening staff at Heligan, this picture was part of the set taken by my grandmother during the winter of 1915-16, which she and my grandfather spent at Heligan.* LEFT Rhododendron arboreum. *One of the many species of rhododendron that Sir Joseph Hooker brought back to England and distributed around various gardens, especially in Cornwall. Growing in tandem with bamboo, this plant could be in Nepal or Sikkim where R. arboreum is a common sight.*

used as shelter in the past, and plenty remained at the start of the restoration. Much of it had perished under the chainsaw through the middle of the garden – laurel is an accomplished poacher of ground and had to be controlled – but a great deal of the original shelter either survived or has been replaced.

In the big Cornish gardens, shelterbelts tended to be established before the garden itself, being placed throughout the area and not just around the circumference. You see this at places like Caerhays, just a few miles down the road from Heligan, where big hedges of laurel run all through the garden, sheltering their National Collection of magnolias and the numerous *Camellia x williamsii* hybrids, for which the Williams family who live there are responsible. The importance of effective shelter is also especially notable on the Isles of Scilly, where the wind is even less merciful as it roars across the rocky outcrops of the archipelago. The tiny fields in which the earliest potatoes and daffodils are grown are protected by huge hedges of *Escallonia* and *Pittosporum crassifolium*, both salt tolerant and wind proof.

When I first arrived at Heligan the Monterey pines that ringed the car park and made up a large part of the eastern shelterbelt were visible from miles around. Sadly, there are few left now, but we have started planting them again for shelter. This tree (*Pinus radiata*) is a native of Monterey in mid California where they are a common sight around Monterey Bay, standing bent and gnarled on the cliff tops, baring their souls to the Pacific Ocean. A remarkable species of tree, but one which sadly has a limited life span of around one hundred and fifty years, it was discovered by the prolific adventurer and plant hunter David Douglas. Once they reach the century mark the trees begin to lose their limbs freely, ending up with a mophead of dark

RIGHT *This couple walking on the petal-strewn path under* Magnolia campbellii *in March were celebrating their golden wedding anniversary with a visit to Heligan. The enormous pink blooms are borne on bare wood and die off before the leaf is produced in the latter part of the spring. The sight of such an enormous tree magnolia is like that of no other plant.*

green pine needles and ragged, bare stumps where once were branches. This conifer can be seen all over Cornwall, where the conditions mimic those in mid and northern California. One consolation for their relatively short life is that the wood burns beautifully, without spitting, emitting that wonderful, resinous scent of pine. Another conifer discovered by Douglas which also found its way to Heligan, and is still with us, is the Douglas fir (introduced in 1827). Spotted by Douglas in Canada, this tree carries an unlikely dwarfing gene, the same as is used in growing bonsai, a trait made evident by a ruff of foliage halfway up its trunk. Douglas, who also gave us the scourge of Scotland, the Sitka spruce (*Picea sitchensis*), perished in

ABOVE *The Mount: gibbet hillock, beacon or lookout post? No satisfactory answer has ever been given as to its origin or purpose. As it is now covered in ferns with a large ash tree growing on top, perhaps the wait will go on.*

a pit dug to trap wild animals; a terrible and rather unfortunate end for a real adventurer who spent year upon year tackling native Indians, smugglers, pirates, thieves and murderers. I have great admiration for the men who, in the mid nineteenth century and before, went to the four corners of the earth in search of plants when not everywhere was painted the red, white and blue of the British Empire. The extraordinary feats of the Scot Robert Fortune in China in the 1840s brought us such wonderful plants as *Lonicera fragrantissima*, the heavily scented winter-flowering honeysuckle, and the chusan palm, *Trachycarpus fortunei*, which is dotted all around the gardens at Heligan. Some, like Fortune, lived out their days in peace, but others like the unfortunate Douglas paid for their efforts dearly. The hardships these great men underwent to shape our environment were enormous, and we are forever in their debt. Whilst the great rhododendrons shape the layout of the pleasure grounds in the Northern Gardens, they were not the first plants to arrive; nor were they the first influence on the landscape.

## The Mount

There are many unexplained things about Heligan; it is from this, for many, that it derives much of its appeal. The 'Mount' is a good example. This little hillock, which lies tight to the northern boundary of the garden at the back of Flora's Green, has never been satisfactorily explained, neither by garden historians nor anyone else. It is about twenty feet high with a spiral pathway to the top. Visitors are discouraged from climbing it to prevent it eroding completely, but if you were to climb it, the only view you would now see would be the oak and beech trees that grow out of its sides.

Dating it is difficult, and suggestions as to its origin and purpose vary. There are several legends attached to the Mount: that it was a viewing platform allowing a pleasant vista over the gardens, or used for spying hostile armadas; that it was part of a chain of beacons, a sort of primitive early-warning system; and lastly, that it was a place of execution. As it is sited on

the highest ground on the estate, any one of those theories could be true. Viewing mounds were popular in the seventeenth and eighteenth centuries, playing a part in the prevailing symbolism with which contemporary gardens were imbued, and many still survive in older gardens today. The Mount was definitely built before the rhododendrons were planted around Flora's Green and which now obscure it. The only trees still standing today which predate it in the Northern Gardens are the two oaks on the eastern side of the Vegetable Garden and the oak on the corner of the Northern Summerhouse. Before the rhododendrons grew tall there would have been a good view out to the south-east coast between the trees. Likewise a fire would have sent a clear signal for miles around along the chain of beacons that were used to pass messages. I find it very difficult to believe that the Mount was in any way used for executions, however. They generally took place on public ground with a large audience in attendance, not on private land. It is a grisly thought.

## The Northern Summerhouse

Like many of its neighbouring gardens in Cornwall, Heligan is somewhat enclosed; this is by both necessity and design, the need for shelter being the governing factor. However, tucked away in the very farthest north-easternmost corner of the garden is the Northern Summerhouse, from where the view is unparalleled. It is almost due east over St Austell Bay to the Gribbin Head with its red and white hooped day mark, and beyond to Rame Head, behind which hides Plymouth, and even, on the clearest of days, to Start Point in Devon. Nestling down on the shore under the Gribbin is the small village of Polkerris, above which are the trees of Menabilly, Monterey pines among them, distinct over five miles away. Home of the Rashleigh family since the sixteenth century and nurturing a fine valley garden of its own, Menabilly was leased to Daphne du Maurier, from where she wrote the majority of her novels. This was the Manderley of *Rebecca*, the house at the top of whose stairs the terrifying Mrs Danvers stood, hands clasped together, to welcome the new Mrs de Winter. This is the view directly up the English Channel towards France. It is the westerly wind which prevails in Cornwall and, thanks to our strong western shelterbelt, it goes across the garden at a good height, overhead and away out to sea. In many ways it is comforting for us gardeners to stand and look out towards the Channel with this wind at our backs, as it reminds us how protected Heligan is. We are well sheltered from the west, but stand at the Northern Summerhouse in an easterly gale and be prepared for a fright. This wind brings salt and sometimes frost; it is often dry, being the result of high pressure, and comes directly from Russia; it is damaging.

At Win Green, an ancient burial site near Shaftesbury in Dorset – a mere 150 miles from Heligan and, at 500 feet above sea level, at precisely the same height – there is a cairn on which a plaque tells you that if you were to take a direct line to the east, the next highest point you would come to would be the Ural Mountains in eastern Russia. All of southern England, Holland, France, Germany and Poland offer nothing to buffer the east wind. This is why it is so cold. The garden around the Northern Summerhouse is framed by a hedge of *Griselinia littoralis*, a very useful shrub in this position because its thick, lime-green glaucous leaves are salt tolerant, making it invaluable. The hedge is cut in a 'U' shape to allow for the view.

The Northern Summerhouse is tended by Mary Crowle. It is Mary, with her helper Trish Hogg, who prunes and ties in the climbing *Rosa* 'Félicité et Perpétue' which sprawls over the summerhouse; and it is Mary who deadheads the two Angels because she knows that there is nothing worse than the dead flowers of a white *Camellia japonica* left on the plant. St Austell born and bred, Mary keeps the pots filled with year-round colour, whether lily-of-the-valley (*Convallaria*) in late spring or African lilies (*Agapanthus*) in high summer. She has seen changes aplenty for the little garden around the Northern Summerhouse. The slate paving around the pond – the finest from the quarries at Delabole on the north coast of Cornwall – used to be grass, but a couple of wet summers and a few thousand pairs of feet saw to that. The path through was once beaten earth, then scalpings, now cobbles. The summerhouse is the oldest structure in the garden and Mary looks after it beautifully, having done so since she came to Heligan in the mid-1990s. Mary has also been responsible for the reintroduction of fantailed doves into the gardens. The first dovecote to be brought back into use is still sited near the great *Magnolia campbellii* in the far north-western corner of the garden, but whilst there the early populations were dogged by attacks from foxes on the ground and sparrowhawks in the air. The sparrowhawk is an extraordinarily agile bird. One of the smallest of the raptors seen in Europe, it is deadly even in the most densely wooded areas, flying low and fast through the trees in pursuit of its prey. The fantails proved to be sitting ducks for the sparrowhawk until Mary finally got the message across: the dovecote had to be moved, or the population would

RIGHT *Shade is cast by the morning sunlight over the pool in front of the Northern Summerhouse by one of the three remaining oaks that are found along the eastern boundary of the garden.* FAR RIGHT *Detail of the dip sculpted into the hedge,* Griselinia littoralis, *on the boundary of the summerhouse garden. The visitor is drawn to admire the stunning view over the farmland to the sea beyond.* OPPOSITE *The view over the hedge to the Gribbin Head and beyond to Pencarrow Head. The very farthest landmark is Rame Head, behind which lie Saltash and Plymouth. The red-roofed barns to the left are Peruppa Farm.*

not burgeon. Now a new dovecote, handmade in our own workshop, is sited on the edge
of the orchard where the poultry live. This is perfect for the fantails, which are sociable birds
and like to be around humans – especially Mary, who treats them as her own. Their cooing
is always a comforting sound in the day-to-day workings of the garden, and their aerial
antics please everyone no end.

Many areas of the garden, for a variety of reasons, have faced minimal interference since
the first slashes of the scythe in 1991. For example, it was quite often decided that areas of
tangled undergrowth so much reflected the look which visitors had come to expect that they
were best left alone. Peering into dense patches of shelterbelt and shrubbery gave people the
impression that this was how the garden had looked before the restoration got under way and
in many cases it was entirely appropriate, therefore, to leave well alone. In others, however,
the time had come to put to rights years of neglect that would never have been permitted
when the garden was at its height. The Ravine is one such example.

## The Ravine

The Ravine was the brainchild of Jack Tremayne, my grandfather's friend, who created an
alpine garden mimicking a European mountain scene. This garden, now returned to its
former glory, presented a significant challenge because its rocky peaks and intricate waterways
were covered in trees – not the ideal companions for alpine plants – which had to be carefully
removed and their roots teased out. It is curious to think of 75-year-old trees in such a way,
but these ash, sycamore and oak, some of which were replanted but many of which were not,

represented giant weeds – plants in the wrong place. The Ravine also underwent a short period as a fernery during the late nineties while the overhead tree canopy was in place; but this did not last, and finally Philip rose to the challenge and declared that it must be an alpine garden. Looking back through history you find that some of the best gardeners professed a weakness for alpine plants. Vita Sackville-West is probably the best example, but there are many others. Helen Dillon, Ireland's number one gardener, broadcaster and writer, whose garden in Sandford Road, Dublin, is out of this world, joined the Alpine Garden Society as a child. Professor Keith Lamb, for many years the most senior figure in Irish horticultural education, has created a truly amazing alpine garden in an old piggery, which lies behind his house on the edge of the great peat bogs in County Offaly.

Behind every alpine garden is a gardener of genius, and Heligan has its very own in Beki Marriott, who looked after the alpine garden at the Birmingham Botanical Garden before coming to us in 2002. Now she floats over the Ravine like a chamois, weeding amongst the various different varieties of *Phlox*, *Helianthemum* and *Pulsatilla* that have created dense drifts and carpets of colour, just as you might see on the scree slopes of the Alps or the Appenines.

## The Italian Garden

Jack Tremayne's European forays also gave rise to the Italian Garden, a small but elegant enclosure, which lies directly beneath the Ravine and shares a west-facing wall with the Melon Yard. This garden, built around 1905, was one of the first areas of Heligan that John Nelson completely restored to something very close to its original size and layout. The summerhouse at the north end is overlooked by one of the more interesting camellias in the garden, *C. oleifera*, and the borders around the pool are now filled with plants such as *Echium*, *Clianthus*, *Euphorbia*, *Cordyline* and *Olea* (olives), which could place this garden anywhere in the Mediterranean.

It is impossible to know just what Jack Tremayne was thinking when he built the Italian Garden, but siting it next to the Ravine was a stroke of genius. To go from a pavilion with a pool and such plants as kiwi fruits, olives and cordylines, to the scree slopes of the high alps and plants that cling to this thin skin by their finger tips, is quite some transformation. Clearly

the two gardens were meant to be together so the comparison could be made, and to that end it is a clever piece of design. To tack the Italian Garden on to the Melon Yard wall was also a bold move; the pavilion, after all, adjoins the thunderbox room, the old lavatory used by the workers. Although there was much less fuss made about things like that in the old days, Jack was still cutting it fine. But then he was running out of room within the confines of the Northern Gardens; the productive gardens had long been built, as had the Crystal Grotto, the Northern Summerhouse and the Sundial Garden.

It may have been that the fernery in the Ravine had become overgrown and past its best. With the alpine garden in the Ravine in place, it would then have been possible to descend the mountain, pass the waterfall and follow the winding path through the woods and into the Italian Garden, just as Jack Tremayne had probably done in Italy.

## New Zealand

One particular plant that inspired the early pioneers of the restoration project – to the extent that it has become the Heligan's 'logo', imprinted on T-shirts, baseball caps and plenty of other merchandise – is the tree fern. *Dicksonia antarctica* was introduced into Cornwall in the 1880s by Treseder's Nurseries, making the journey as ballast on ships from south-eastern Australia. The plants then found their way into the county's numerous large gardens and proved very popular, enjoying the climate that mimicked that of home. The earliest to arrive at Heligan were probably those at the very bottom of the Jungle, the valley garden that stretches away beneath Heligan House towards the sea at Mevagissey. Later arrivals were planted in the area that we now call New Zealand, a slip of a garden that hides to the east of the Vegetable Garden and merges with a great Victorian relic, the Crystal Grotto. The abundance of tree ferns allowed for the creation of an entire garden filled with plants from the Antipodes and the number of species of tree fern has now risen to five: *Dicksonia antarctica*, *D. fibrosa* and *D. squarrosa*, the extraordinary black-trunked *Cyathea medullaris*, and *C. dealbata*, which has a silver underside to its leaves and is the fern emblem on the jerseys of the New Zealand rugby team. These great tree ferns flourish in the warm, damp climate of Cornwall

OPPOSITE PAGE *Vibrant red heads of* Rhododendron arboreum, *in full flower in the New Zealand garden. The cobbled drains which have been reinstated are visible to the left. They are the saviour of the paths during the wet Cornish winters.* RIGHT *Cordyline indivisa, one of the most startling Antipodean plants in the garden. This year a wren nested and successfully reared a brood of chicks in the lower leaves, right by the path.* FAR RIGHT *The beautiful Chatham Island forget-me-not* (Myosotidium hortensia), *with its extraordinary blue flowers and glossy, ribbed foliage.*

and throw dappled sunlight through their huge rough fronds, complementing perfectly the surrounding camellias and lower-growing ferns that make up the understorey of plants.

Another great crowd pleaser is the Chatham Island forget-me-not (*Myosotidium hortensia*). So frequent are the questions as to the identification of this plant that the office staff put it in their top ten spring queries from visitors. Although the glossy, ribbed foliage might be mistaken for that of bergenia, there is no mistaking the big heads of vibrant, light blue flowers which are produced on a nine-inch long stem in the spring. It is a beautiful specimen and as a prolific seeder, like all forget-me-nots, it has spread throughout the New Zealand garden. In the same family as the garden forget-me-not (Boraginaceae), this bolder cousin, the only species in its genus, is a native of the Chatham Islands which lie 500 miles to the east of New Zealand in the Pacific Ocean. It seems to thrive in the leaf litter that makes up the floor of the shrubbery that is New Zealand, sheltering from any frost in the lee of the tree ferns with a little help from a straw mulch. It clashes superbly with the varying reds of the camellias and rhododendrons amongst which it is planted.

The New Zealand garden has been carefully managed and planned over the last few years by Mike Friend, who has made it his business to learn as much as possible about the plants that he has been growing. He has put together an impressive collection of ferns to go with the tall *Dicksonia*, some of which have reached over twenty feet in height. The bigger ones have allowed saprophytic plants to get a hold in their thick fibrous stems; stray seeds of beech, *Rhododendron ponticum* and *Uncinia rubra*, a red grass with barbed seeds, can be seen growing happily on the

PREVIOUS PAGE *The spiky fronds of* Astelia chathamica *are seen here in the New Zealand garden, mixed up with an ever-increasing population of Chatham Island forget-me-nots* (Myosotidium hortensia). *The bent tree fern in the middle of the picture was probably inhibited by rampant under- and overgrowth.*

RIGHT Clematis indivisa. *One of the most startling of all the clematis species, this plant has started to colonise the garden. The flowers stand upright on long, thin stems in a most unusual fashion.* ABOVE *Bergenias thrive in the moist and slightly acidic soils at Heligan. There is a good colony underneath an ancient* Rhododendron falconeri *by the Flower Garden.* LEFT *A very handsome stand of* Libertia grandiflora. *These clumps flower in early summer, and bloom continuously well into the autumn.*

PREVIOUS PAGE *The path between the Crystal Grotto and Wishing Well. In the shady, moisture-laden atmosphere, the rockery, untouched for so many years, is now completely covered in moss. Foxgloves, ferns and bamboo grow in tiny pockets of soil between the stones.* LEFT *The route out of the Crystal Grotto is hindered by a fallen* Rhododendron arboreum. *It is this willingness to*

*leave alone that has added so much atmosphere and romance to the garden.* ABOVE *Only when it rains heavily is there anything other than twelve inches of crystal clear water in the cavern of the Wishing Well. It is an eerie place.* RIGHT *Once lined with flashing crystals and lit with candles at night, the Crystal Grotto must have oozed romance, even for the Victorians. Damp and must have replaced crystal and candle, but the resonance remains.*

tree ferns. The garden is sheltered from its neighbour to the west, the Vegetable Garden, by a line of *Pseuodopanax arboreus*, a tree much used as shelter on the Isles of Scilly. The New Zealand garden also boasts three magnificent *Magnolia grandiflora* 'Gallisoniensis', a slightly different variety to the magnolias in the Sundial Garden. It is a treat to see these evergreen trees free-standing. They are most often trained against walls but they can reach a huge size, as anyone who has seen them growing in the south-eastern United States will testify. Once bigger, they will make a good ally to the *M. delavayi,* which is an original planting in the same area; the orange scent of the flowers through summer and autumn should be intense. The development of New Zealand has been the perfect counter to the shadowy eeriness of the Crystal Grotto, which it adjoins.

## The Crystal Grotto and Wishing Well

The Crystal Grotto has remained virtually untouched since restoration work began. Once lined with huge lumps of quartz crystal, the rocky dell that surrounds it is overhung with tree ferns and huge specimens of *Rhododendron arboreum.* It is dark and heavily atmospheric. The massive luxulyanite boulders that surround the Crystal Grotto and the Wishing Well are covered in dark green moss and lichen from the constant drip of the overhead tree canopy over the past hundred years. These huge stones come from seven or eight different sources in the Luxulyan Valley, just to the east of St Austell. If you did not know its makers were Victorian gardeners – and therefore capable of anything – you might wonder how it was

done, or ask what race of people had been able to pile up such outsize rocks, one on top of another. The Wishing Well boasts the sweetest water in the garden, which pumps up into it from a spring; the workers who heaved those vast stones surely drank from it.

The well is an ancient structure, something which can be felt standing in front of it, imagining how our forebears drank and drew their water. It is marked on a 1777 plan of the garden and that makes it venerable indeed. It is easy to imagine our predecessors taking moonlit walks late at night and sitting quietly in the grotto, with the sparkling light from the candles reflecting off the crystals. Occasionally, when clearing up after a theatre on Flora's Green, or when the garden has been open in the evening for a Friends of Heligan event, these scenes come to mind. But the tendency is to blow out the candles and hurry on home; you never quite know who is watching you in that dark, quiet place with its thick air and dank, musty smell. It takes you back to the Victorian way of life, to thoughts of those who worked the land, or down in the tin mines, or out at sea in the pilchard fleets. The rain-sodden south-westerly wind can drive a man to distraction through the dark days of a Cornish winter. It creeps into every nook and cranny and seeps into the bones of the hardiest of gardeners. Whether it is a full gale or the mizzle that lifts in silently off the sea, there is no escaping the Cornish climate. And yet it nourishes trees and shrubs and staves off

ABOVE *My grandmother, usually the photographer, inspects the sundial and checks to see if it tells the right time. The sundial was removed to the front of Heligan House not long after this picture was taken in 1915.*

the ravages of a dry summer; it can be soft and full of moisture, too, when walking the high-hedged, sheltered lanes of the county.

During the wet winter months a considerable amount of water passes through the garden. The Wishing Well, a small cave dug below ground level, is a natural collecting point. The water brings with it a quantity of silt which collects in the well. The drop in altitude from the top of the garden at Flora's Green to the bottom at the Sundial Garden is quite severe, and the drains and soakaways have to be checked regularly for silt and debris to avoid floods. This task is carried out with great precision by Charles Fleming with the aid of a set of draining rods. The work involved in emptying the well last year was doubled by the amount of coinage mixed up in the silt. Old habits die hard; it is nice to know that wishing wells still live up to their name.

## The Sundial Garden

Although the Sundial Garden lies directly beneath the Flower Garden, it never had a role as a productive garden. The herbaceous border that lies against its south-facing wall was described in the *Gardener's Chronicle* of 1896 as 'the finest herbaceous border in England', and this garden was almost certainly always used for ornamental horticulture.  From the earliest times of the

BELOW *The sundial now stands proudly in its former position, in the middle of the lawn in the Sundial Garden. It was reinstated in 1996 after being kindly released by the residents of Heligan House. It is exactly the same as it ever was, except for the new base on which it rests.*

restoration it became obvious that there was only a handful of noteworthy plants left from Victorian plantings; the borders had disappeared under mounds of bramble, rough grass and the ubiquitous seedling weed trees.

Two plants stood out in particular, both climbers and both still very much worthy of their place in the garden today but, like many things, they are proving difficult to manage in their old age. One is a truly wonderful *Wisteria sinensis,* which winds itself around the stone gate posts, and the second is a *Stauntonia hexaphylla,* which grows up the first bay of the south-facing wall. There is also a *Magnolia grandiflora* 'Exmouth' on the north-facing wall of the Sundial Garden. This old plant still produces its huge, cup-shaped flowers in midsummer; and the slight scent of orange in the overpowering fragrance is almost too much to bear. There are three *M. grandiflora* planted on the north-facing wall of the Flower Garden and we have planted three more *M. grandiflora* 'Gallisoniensis' in the area between the Vegetable Garden and the Eastern Ride. It is there that one of our few other remaining magnolias resides. Lying on its side, but still full of life, is a very old *M. x soulangeana* 'Lennei' which produces beautiful goblet-shaped purple flowers in late spring and early summer. The south-facing wall of the Sundial Garden is home to numerous other climbers such as *Actinidia kolomikta, Trachelospermum asiaticum* and *T. jasminoides,* but it is the *Stauntonia hexaphylla* and the *Wisteria sinensis* that hold our hearts. In early spring 2003 the *Stauntonia,* which had reached the top of the wall and was still growing vigorously, finally came away, pulling its nails and wires out of the wall as it did so. The decision was taken to cut it back to a few buds, a brave one considering the age of the plant and its place in the history of the garden. Then the cold weather came. Not frost, but east wind – for day after day through March, April and May. The wind shredded the handkerchief tree (*Davidia involucrata*) at the top of the Sundial Garden, and it anaesthetised the young flower buds of the statuesque *Rhododendron falconeri* outside the Head Gardener's Office, to the extent that the buds never burst; the plant did not flower. All through that time there was no movement from the *Stauntonia;* our hearts were in our mouths. Finally in June, as the weather warmed up, so did the soil, and when the rain came the old *Stauntonia* sprang to life as if a good haircut and a lengthy spring sleep were just the tonic it needed for rejuvenation.

The great herbaceous border, 100 feet in length, was designed by Chris Gardner with help from his friend, the garden historian Toby Musgrave. It was Toby who had discovered the quotes about the border in the *Gardener's Chronicle* of 1896 and Chris was then given the brief to design the border in a pre-Gertrude Jekyll style. It is abundant throughout the summer months and we are fortunate to be able to grow some of the slightly less hardy types of plant with the help of the south-facing wall. *Melianthus major,* for example, is not known by all the visitors with an interest in herbaceous plants. Its silvery foliage reaches an enormous height and the red flower that appears in spring is a surprise to many. But there are more here than just the tender perennials. *Campanula lactiflora* has a lot of admirers, as has the relation of sea kale, *Crambe cordifolia.* There is *Sanguisorba obtusa* with its red spikes, and the blousy white *Romneya coulteri.* The deep purple *Rosa* 'Russelliana' keeps watch over the border from the middle bay of the wall. The border in the Sundial Garden is indeed a spectacular sight. Being the last garden to be finished in the early years of the restoration, it was fitting that its opening fell exactly 100 years on from its mention in horticultural history.

*Everything was perfect: a gentle, southerly slope, impeccable topsoil at least eighteen inches deep with barely a stone in it – they had all been cleared off by apprentice gardeners many years ago – and good shelter on all sides, yet very little shade.*

# Productive
# Heligan

There is no greater joy than that inspired by an abundant kitchen garden. Each has its own atmosphere and particular smell, each its own successes and failures. The continuity appeals so much; other areas in gardens change over time but the kitchen garden remains, solid and dependable in its presence and its continuous production of crops. The intensity of work and devotion to duty that these places inspire is astonishing, the skill with which an apple is grafted or a bunch of grapes thinned, spellbinding. Heligan's productive gardens are no exception.

## The Vegetable Garden

There is one double-stemmed western red cedar (*Thuja plicata*) left from the original hedge that sheltered the Vegetable Garden from the northerly wind. Well over thirty feet high, it stands in the north-west corner next to the Ravine and rocks perilously in a high westerly wind. This great tree, whose forebears were the giants of the early American paper industry, has overseen much labour in the Vegetable Garden over the centuries; it must be pleased with the result, as the soil in this garden has been left in its ideal state. I first started work at Heligan in 1993, the same year that John Nelson had reclaimed a substantial section of the Vegetable Garden and begun to tend it. How can I ever forget the sight of Charles Fleming down on his knees lifting potatoes? The man has worn out so many pairs of kneeling pads he must hold a record. Since then the garden has changed many times in both size and shape. In the autumn of 1993 one

of my first tasks was to deal with the remainder of the encroaching laurel that had swamped its western flank. By that time the young ash and sycamore trees and the bramble that had colonised the garden had been removed, most of the soil was clear and the paths were falling back into place. The garden was well on its way to revival.

The difficult decision as to which trees should remain, and which should not, had been a serious issue from day one, and it became even more so as we began to reclaim ground for cultivation. One ancient apple tree was overgrown, fruiting poorly and generally in a lamentable condition, with severe canker. It hung over the path by the door through to the Melon Yard, the frame yard which adjoins the Vegetable Garden to the south. Finally, after much agonising, it was removed. In 1995 another very large tree, this time an ash, was removed from the south-eastern corner of the Vegetable Garden, a few yards from where the compost heaps are now situated. That tree cast morning shadow on the garden and trapped a lot of humidity. This led to regular problems with fungal diseases – such as blight on potatoes and mildew on onions – so the decision was taken to remove it. Our onions were fine down there last year, but we lost our entire garlic crop, over one hundred feet of row length, to an unspecified fungal attack. Similarly, there was a small group of self-sown ash trees that had sited themselves directly beneath the south-facing walls of the Melon Yard. Seventy-five years of growth in warm south-west England can produce a large tree, and these again cast a lot of shade, this time over a yard in which young plants are raised for the Vegetable Garden. They, too, had to be removed.

The resurgence of this enormous garden was immensely pleasurable to all who worked it in those days. Over an acre of vegetables was under cultivation by the spring of 1994, including many of the same varieties grown in the same manner as they were when the gardens were at

*The blue-green leeks, Musselburgh and Carentan, Scottish and French, are the winter foot-soldiers of the Vegetable Garden. They line up like infantry in their ranks and repel the soaking rains of winter with great pluck.*

their zenith in the middle of the nineteenth century. This was a genuine tribute to all of those fantastically skilled men and boys who viewed horticulture as an art form, and possessed growing skills that are far less in evidence today. To them, the grafting of an apple scion on to a rootstock, or the budding of a rose, was second nature. For me it is an honour to follow in the footsteps of those who grew grapes, peaches, potatoes and carrots, not to mention the finest pineapples in the south of England. In these days of instant gardening, cultivation is a word used less and less. It has several meanings, primarily referring to the growing of crops and plants, but also to the preparation and care of the ground to promote their growth. To make a success of the job in hand we had, and still have, to cultivate the garden.

The decision, then, to work this garden as the Victorians would have done was a bold one, but one which nevertheless was soon to pay big dividends. To begin with, it meant that everything had to be done by hand; the preparation of the ground and the maintenance of its highest level of fertility were to be done without the use of machinery. Mechanisation was just coming into play in Victorian times; the furthest they came to using it to cultivate the Vegetable Garden might have been the use of a pony to draw a plough. I have lost count of the amount of tiny horseshoes that I have come across when turning or grading the soil. People often enquire of us: 'Are you still finding things?' The answer is always yes, but in some cases we are still looking. I am still trying to decipher which of the last remaining buildings next to the Poultry Yard was the one that housed the pony. I do know, however, that next to the building that I suspect was the stable is what used to be the lime store. On our slightly acidic soil in Cornwall, lime is an essential ingredient in soil fertility – particularly where the brassica, or cabbage, family is concerned. You can be certain that a garden such as Heligan would have grown a large amount of cabbages, Brussels sprouts, kale, cauliflowers, spring greens, turnips, radishes or any other member of that family. It is an extensive family and would have represented a large proportion of the 'greens' that were relied upon for vitamins and minerals in the Victorian diet, particularly through the long, strength-sapping winter. Without a similar level of fertility, nothing would be possible. So we picked up where the Victorians left off, with the main difference that we had to find the manure to feed the soil from elsewhere, whereas theirs came directly from the estate's stable yard.

To understand what was required of the Vegetable Garden it is necessary to look back at how lives were led one hundred and fifty years ago – particularly those of a family like the Tremaynes, their employees and their friends and, even more importantly, how it all happened in Cornwall. The 'disposable' society in which we live today bears little or no resemblance to that inhabited by the Victorians. Yet as we pretend to strive for a cleaner, greener planet we would do well to try and understand the way things were then. Heligan was probably a fairly good example of a self-sustaining estate, a viable model in those days, one might imagine, if in the hands of responsible owners who spurned the gaming tables of London, the bookmakers and the bottle. It would have been difficult to indulge in these things at Heligan, however, given the remote location of Cornwall, far from what is still joked about in these parts as 'civilisation'. As it happened, the Tremaynes were, by and large, responsible to themselves, their employees and their lands. The Vegetable Garden played a key role in terms of self-sufficiency. A household of prominence such as Heligan rose and fell on the quality of the company, the entertainment and the food. With bad roads, and imports not as widespread as they are today, most produce had to be home-grown, and for this the cook looked to the head gardener.

With guidance from Peter Thoday, our foremost expert on garden history and architecture (producer of the excellent *The Victorian Kitchen Garden* series for BBC Television), it soon became clear to Tim, John and Philip that the walled gardens at Heligan were very fine indeed and that restoration to full working order was the next step. By the spring of 1994 the Vegetable Garden was in full production and for the next three seasons the vast majority of my time was spent in there, cultivating the enormous range of fruits, vegetables and cut flowers that would have been expected of me had I been the head gardener in the Victorian era. It was a dream come true. I was right back there at the Porthpean of my childhood, clinging to old Pope's apron strings – except this time it was me pollinating peaches, or wrapping celery in brown paper to keep it blonde and sweet. It was like a huge adventure playground, complete with an enormous range of glasshouses that were soon to be restored, working to full capacity. To take out a trench and plant 100 feet of asparagus, or to work in a completely refurbished, early nineteenth-century glasshouse entirely devoted to the cultivation of cucumbers and melons, were truly exceptional possibilities.

## The Soil

The soil is the foundation of the range of crops in the productive gardens at Heligan, and to keep it in the best possible health the gardens are worked on a rotational basis – as they would have been at their inception. This is the practice of moving annual plants around the garden by family each year, and is still the best way to improve soil fertility and prevent the build-up of pests and diseases, especially those of a soil-borne nature. Today's arable soils that produce the world's grains and vegetables no longer nourish plants the way they used to. They are used merely as rooting mechanisms while the plants are fed with cocktails of artificial nutrients for growth, and prophylactic fungicides and pesticides to combat pests and diseases. How this method can possibly produce wholesome food is beyond me. To grow a healthy plant you have to have a healthy soil, and the best way to do that is to feed the soil and understand its requirements.

Soil is more than simply what the Americans call dirt. It is made up of invertebrates (big, such as earthworms, and small, such as microscopic nematode worms), yeasts, fungi, bacteria, organic matter and stones, the weathering of which over the ages is largely where it came from in the first place. We cannot possibly hope to grow strong plants in soil without

feeding it because all those ingredients need food to survive (except the stones, of course). If you take as much out of your soil as we do, in the form of fruits and vegetables, then provision must be made for the return of nourishment for the next crop.

The rotation works as follows. In the first season potatoes (Solanaceae) are planted, the plot for which is double dug with well-rotted manure incorporated in the bottom of the trench. After the potatoes are dug through the summer, their place is taken by the winter brassicas (Brassiceae), that is to say Brussels sprouts, sprouting broccoli, cabbages, kales and cauliflowers. Potatoes are very hungry and need bulk feeding; cabbages do not, so the remnants of the horse manure left over by the potatoes will suffice for them. The following season the greens make way for the root crops (Umbelliferae) such as parsnips, carrots, scorzonera, salsify and Hamburg parsley (root parsley). In the third season the ground, which by this time is somewhat depleted of nitrogen, is planted with peas and beans (Leguminosae). It is one of nature's many miracles that these leguminous crops are able to store atmospheric nitrogen and release it to help nourish themselves and other plants as required. After the peas and beans come the garlic, onions, shallots and leeks (Alliaceae), which gladly use up the nitrogen left over from the legumes. The plot is then double dug again, with manure incorporated, to make ready for the following year's crop of pumpkins, squashes and gourds (Cucurbitaceae). The final course of the rotation is a 'bits and pieces' section which holds the crops that don't fit into the regime, such as one or two summer brassicas (namely kohlrabi and a crop of summer cabbages and cauliflowers), celery, celeriac, dwarf French beans for drying, the chards and perpetual spinach. This system takes up the main sections on four sides of a cruciform path that dissects the Vegetable Garden. All the cultivation is done by hand: the winter digging,

the spring preparation, the grading to the correct level and the summer weeding, for which no herbicides have ever been used. In addition, there are large sections of soft fruit, summer flower bulbs, cut flower beds, a two-bed strawberry rotation, a perennial vegetable section, which comprises globe artichokes, cardoons, Jerusalem artichokes and two asparagus beds, and a mature apple arch which runs from the top to the bottom of the garden. To manage nearly two acres of fruit and vegetables on an intensive scale such as this is an enormous labour of love, and the only way to do it is to have the highest possible level of soil fertility. This comes from tons of horse manure manhandled from the Pineapple Pit each year, all dug in by hand with a Cornish shovel and a lot of Cornish beef (in the substantial forms of Clive Mildenhall and Mike Rundle). The pièce de résistance is the seaweed, which in the autumn is brought from Portmellon Beach (the next cove around the coast to the west of Mevagissey), and spread thickly over bare soil wherever possible. Whilst it is not especially high in the big three nutrients of nitrogen, phosphate and potash (although it does add some of the trace elements), it does fulfil an important role as a soil conditioner, and is a means of preventing soil erosion and nutrient loss during the heavy winter rains. Despite the programme of feeding that the soil receives, it is still hungry enough for a four-inch layer of seaweed to disappear completely over a period of three months. All that is left behind are various bits of detritus, as well as non-biodegradable by-products of the petro-chemical industry and other unmentionables.

If you take a lot out of a garden you have to put plenty back, otherwise the system breaks down. The result of all this digging and seaweed-spreading is a robust and healthy soil. It can grow anything, and can aid the plants which grow in it to withstand attacks from pests and diseases, the cycles of which are inhibited by the simple act of rotating the crops. This way of gardening was firmly in place in the Victorian era and I doubt that the way we cultivate the garden now is much different from the way it was done then. The fruits of our labours end up in the kitchens, but not those of the house; they go to the tea room to nourish the visitors.


## The Organic Question

'Are you organic?' is one of the questions most frequently asked by visitors to the garden. It is an emotive issue and one that bears careful thought. Mike Rundle talks about a traditional rather than organic method of gardening when asked this question. I have often heard him painstakingly explain to visitors how plants are much better able to withstand attacks from pests and diseases if they are grown in a strong, healthy and fertile soil rather than being reliant on chemicals for their growth. There is not much Mike can't tell you about the soil in the Vegetable Garden; he has spent ten winters digging it.

During the years in which I was absent from Heligan, 1997–2001, I grew fruit and vegetables certified organic under rules laid down by the country's premier certification body, the Soil Association. At Heligan we use a fungicide for the prevention of potato blight and occasionally, in wet seasons, a chemical to control slugs. Whilst I am organic by nature, I have a garden to run and a great many visitors to please. With this in mind I take heart from the father of the Permaculture movement, the Australian Bill Mollison, who said if a chemical has to be used, then use it, only don't make a habit of it.

We have never been in the habit of using artificial fertiliser on the ground to feed the crops, although lime, in the form of calcified seaweed, is applied after the potatoes are removed and before the winter brassicas (cabbages, cauliflowers, etc.) are planted in their place. Lime is a soil 'sweetener', maintaining the balance of the soil and allowing plants to take up the nutrients supplied by the compost or manure. It has also been used for centuries to raise the pH level of the soil, that is, the degree of acidity or alkalinity, and therefore keep the club root fungus, which attacks all members of the brassica tribe, inactive.

Funny stuff is soil. It does not simply give the plant what it wants as a matter of course; certain elements like iron, for example, can get 'locked up' if conditions are not favourable, while potash is very soluble in water and gets easily washed out or leached by heavy rain. Even our use of calcified seaweed, an entirely natural product permitted for use under Soil Association rules, can have its drawbacks. Our soils in Cornwall generally, and at Heligan specifically, err on the acid side of neutral. The higher the pH the more likely the

*BELOW If only there were so many more. Every year great lines of frog spawn float in the pool in the Italian Garden, and then the signs have to go up: 'Beware baby frogs crossing'. Apart from being delightful, frogs and toads are deadly to slugs, and should be encouraged for that reason alone.*

presence of scab, a very undesirable fungal disease in the potato crop. Since scab is only ever found on potatoes that are grown in soils of a high pH, there is a strong possibility that the calcified seaweed is inducing scab on our potatoes.

As if that were not enough for the potato crop to cope with, there is still the biggest problem of all: potato blight. The greatest curse of all for potato growers, this clever fungus was responsible for the potato famine in Ireland which killed a million people in 1846–7 and is still prevalent today. It must also surely have come to the notice of the anti-GM lobby, given that one of the main reasons for the scourge of blight through the Irish crop nearly

two centuries ago was that only one variety of potato was grown. This is the strategy of the biotechnology companies: to encourage the growth of one variety at the expense of diversity, the result of which is no escape route in times of disaster.

In the 1870s it was discovered that a chemical fungicide made up of a mixture of copper sulphate and slaked lime was an effective preventive treatment for mildew on vines in France. By the turn of the century the same Bordeaux Mixture – as it was known – was in use against potato blight. Spraying fortnightly from the middle of May to the end of August with this treatment was reasonably effective at Heligan until 1998, when it rained so much that the Bordeaux Mixture barely had time to settle on the leaves before the rain washed it off. The result was that, in the warm and humid conditions perfect for the spread of blight, the disease tore through the crop, reducing the foliage of the potatoes to brown stubs and the tubers to stinking mush – the same scene that spelled starvation for the Irish peasants in 1846. For us it meant crop failure and the loss of heritage varieties carefully collected over the years.

After I returned to Heligan in 2000 I started to notice scab on potatoes for the first time, and whilst I cannot be sure whether this was due to too much calcified seaweed or Bordeaux Mixture, I do know that the Soil Association, the most prominent organic certification body in the country, has severely restricted the use of Bordeaux Mixture because of the build-up of copper in soils. Rather, they advocate the use of blight-resistant varieties and wider spacing between the rows of the crop.

One alternative means of control is the systemic fungicide, where a chemical is drawn into the entire system of the plant, thereby making it impervious to the action of the blight fungus. The fungicide breaks down on contact with the soil – but what does this inorganic chemical do to our bodies? In her excellent book *Kitchen Pharmacy* (Orion, 1991) Rose Elliot points out that the cells of the human body are organic, as are those of the food we eat. The body is not designed to absorb inorganic matter; it thus follows that neither the chemicals, nor the plants sprayed with them, are recognised by our bodies. The result of this, she goes on to say, is a build-up of inorganic chemicals, which leads to problems of toxicity. Each year potato blight seems to become even more complex in its chemistry, and conventional growers are on weekly spraying regimes against it. Think what that is doing to the nation's chips.

We are not able to call the garden organic because of the use of this chemical to control blight. Because we spray our maincrop and salad potatoes with systemic fungicide, we are no different from the majority of commercial potato growers in the country, and this is a great pity. If we want to show the varieties of potato that were grown in the garden pre-1910, then we have no choice. This raises the question of how the Victorians managed to control blight. After all, we know from Ireland that the disease was very much in evidence at that time. We also know that a lack of space led maincrop potatoes to be grown on the farm rather than in the enclosed spaces of the vegetable and walled gardens. This would certainly have allowed for wider spacing of rows and more room between plants, thus avoiding the close, clammy and humid conditions that are perfect for the spread of blight. Organic certification bodies also suggest growing disease-resistant varieties, but it it is doubtful whether many were in evidence pre-1910. Certainly, there appears to be almost no resistance to late blight in the varieties that we have grown: the likes of Golden Wonder and Pink Fir Apple are very susceptible to it.

The use of a fungicide for blight and an occasional purge of the slug population make us look angelic in comparison to the Victorians, who were ruthless in their application of deadly chemicals. Arsenic, tobacco and sulphur were three commonly used poisons. Beyond this, the way we manage the soil is largely the same as the way the Victorians did: by the consistent application of organic matter and the rotation of crops.

It is important that we understand what happens when we use a chemical and how it interferes with the natural life cycles that make up a healthy farm or garden. It is very hard to make a case for the use of a chemical, even in extreme circumstances, and it is impossible if you wish to call your garden organic. An organic garden or farm must be a holistic unit, where only the minimum of outside influence should be relied upon. The life cycles of plants, pests, diseases, soils and even compost heaps should all be seen in their wider context, as working together as one. The issue of whether or not to use chemicals is a very difficult one, but it pales in comparison to the explosion of genetically modified crops that is on our doorstep.

## Potatoes

It is hard to know precisely which varieties of potato were grown at Heligan a hundred years ago. Suffice it to say that maincrop varieties would have been grown on a huge scale, but on the farm rather than in the garden. First earlies, second earlies and salad potatoes were grown in profusion as a staple for the family and their guests. There was no fancy food for

the workers – the gardeners would have had gardens attached to their cottages and grown whatever they could for themselves. The household servants, who would have taken their meals in the servants' hall at Heligan House, had no gardens in which to grow anything and thereby extend their meagre diet.

Our old potatoes, which all predate 1910, have become widely known as 'heritage' varieties and generate interest because many are as good, and often better, than modern introductions. Take the King Edward for example. The descendent of the great Beauty of Hebron, it is the parent of many fine potatoes, including a good second early called Kestrel. It is versatile to the extent that it can be grown as a second early or a main crop, it roasts, boils, chips and mashes very well, and as such is still a popular commercial variety. It is susceptible to potato blight, but then so are most. This raises the question of how an organic potato grower in the south of England could manage without chemical assistance, when potato blight is still endemic – or should he diversify, as the government tells him that he ought to?

With the potatoes cleared, the winter brassicas are planted in their place, and they pave the way for a whole new lesson in pest control. In the rotation, potatoes and winter brassicas occupy the same ground in the first season and are followed by the root crops in the second.

## Brassicas: Of Cabbages and Kings

The growing of vegetables to the standards we have set is more than a labour of love; it is an art form, and one that Kathy Cartwright has made her own. No one crop has more care and attention than another, but the brassicas are very demanding, almost as much so as the peas. They are not hard to grow but they are hard to grow well. Kathy and I have laughed long and hard about what it takes to put this huge Vegetable Garden together in any one season, the successes and the inevitable failures coming from new and often unexpected sources. The lives of the gardeners through the years have been hard, and failures were not tolerated. In the nineteenth century agricultural and horticultural workers put in long hours, every moment of the day spent on ensuring that all went according to plan. The cabbage tribe is one crop which requires particular attention to detail and great care to produce the necessary results.

A good example is purple sprouting broccoli, a crop from which a lot was expected in a Victorian dining room, and which remains today one of the best of all vegetables. Around the base of each plant is placed a six-by-six-inch square of roofing felt to prevent any lingering cabbage root flies from hatching out into grubs, eating into the roots and killing the plant. Next the row of plants is covered by a long net to keep the woodpigeons off. These normally canny and suspicious individuals are so used to seeing large numbers of people (and probably being fed by many of them) that they have become just like the feral pigeons of Hyde Park: tame. It is easy to imagine what would happen if the broccoli were left uncovered: an open invitation to feast on a favourite crop. So they stay covered until well into September, when the plants are too big for the fat pigeons. All well so far; late July, however, brings another brassica fancier on to the scene. The grub of the cabbage white butterfly has an insatiable appetite for cabbage leaves and, like the pigeon and the potato blight, if not stopped will do terminal damage to the crop. So, just as the old head gardener would have done, we too look at new ways of controlling pests.

In recent years a lot of progress has been made in the field of biological controls. This is based on the idea that one insect controls another – just as in the natural scheme of things, but where a deliberate increase in the population of the predator acts as the means of pest control. In the case of cabbage white larvae the controlling agent is not another insect but a bacteria. A horrific concept – biological warfare in the plant world – and the effects on the pest are devastating. A fortnightly spray of the bacteria, assuming it makes contact with the grubs, will remove the problem. No inorganic chemicals needed, this bacteria is present in the soil. The plants grow on through the late summer and autumn, looking good and preparing themselves for winter. The brassica is a hardy soul (as the names of cauliflowers like Snowball and the cabbage January King will testify), but when a heavy frost sits down on top of the broccoli the plants can look a sorry sight. We wait and we wait until the spring comes, and then suddenly there they are: little purple flower heads in the axils between the stems and the leaves. It is one of the greatest vegetable delicacies of them all, to be compared with asparagus, globe artichokes and sea kale. What a wait it has been: nine to ten months, all that work, all that effort and all that risk, but the first melting shoots on the tongue, smothered in butter, make it all worthwhile. The upshot of all Kathy's toil on the brassica patch are crops that are rarely seen on a garden scale, blemish-free and presentable to the kitchens of The Willows Tea Room.

It says something for Kathy and for our soil that we are able to grow winter cauliflowers. Cauliflowers are like I was at the age of six: fussy. They don't want this, they don't like that, too much of one thing makes them grow too much leaf and too little of another distorts the head. Trace elements, the chemical elements that are present in the soil in much smaller quantities than the big three of nitrogen, phosphate and potash, are what cauliflowers need, and they get the boron and the molybdenum from the seaweed that we haul from the beach at Portmellon. As we heave the seaweed on to the trailer for Mike to pull back with the tractor, like so many of our tasks, it is a trip back in time. Although the use of raw seaweed in agriculture and horticulture is now confined to the far reaches of the Celtic map – in such places as the west of Ireland and the Hebridean, Orkney and Shetland Islands of Scotland – it was once the premier source of soil nutrition. In the years between the wars it was so heavily relied upon that some of the soils of crofting communities on the Scottish Isles became overburdened.

The annual seaweed haul is an autumn activity dependent on more than a little local knowledge. The stretch of coastline between the Gribbin Head and the Dodman Point, which comprises St Austell and Mevagissey Bays, faces east towards France. With a high spring tide and an easterly wind can come vast quantities of seaweed, as the big winds and swells wash any loose weed away from the rocks and push it up on to the shore. There are Lettuces and Wracks and long thick strands of Sea Belts, Furbelows and Tangles, Dulses, Lavers and Sea Thongs.

They all come up in a massive, sandy knot of nutritional goodness and get dumped on to the soil in a four-inch layer. Within three days they have acquired a bleached crust, and after five a considerable whiff of decaying organic matter complete with sand fleas, lice and maggots. By this stage the visitors begin to ask what the appalling smell is, but after a fortnight it has reduced to a faint whiff of the ocean. In three months all that is left of the seaweed is fishing line and old bits of rope. The salt has no damaging effect – as I regularly have to point out to people – and the good that the seaweed does to the soil is immeasurable. There are only four places where soil builds naturally. One is the forest floor, another is under still water, a third is under permanent pasture and the fourth is under a mulch, although this is dependent upon human intervention. There is certainly no better mulch than seaweed. It leaves the soil conditioned to perfection, it builds up its structure and adds the trace elements; it protects it from the winter rains and prevents the leaching of its nutrients; it keeps the soil cool and protects the life within it.

Of all the activities that take place during the gardening year, this is the one that brings the old gardeners up close. You can see them toiling over the vast expanse of the Vegetable Garden, huffing and puffing over huge piles of seaweed, with pipes in the corners of their mouths, longing for crib time and a mouthful of pasty. Seaweed makes an excellent mulch for all the brassicas and puts the soil in tip-top condition for the following year's crop of carrots, which do not require heavy doses of nitrogen.

## Root Crops

One of the biggest challenges for those who garden without general recourse to chemicals is to grow carrots without interference from the dastardly carrot fly. The fly lays its eggs in the soil close to carrots and the larvae tunnel into them, feeding as they go and rendering the carrots inedible. If you grow carrots you will certainly get a visit from the carrot fly, and whilst there are various remedies, not many of them fit that well with what might have happened in Victorian times. The irony of the situation is that the Victorians would almost certainly have reached for some heinous chemical. Our predecessors were not remotely afraid to use them – arsenic, nicotine and sulphur were applied liberally, and not for nothing were the brass spray pumps on display in the Tool Shed in the Melon Yard known as 'widow makers'. Many a gardener fell foul of the appalling levels of toxicity of the chemicals used.

Nowadays, the use of horticultural fleece to cover the carrot crop, or the placement of barriers around the crop (for some unknown reason the carrot fly only flies at just above ground level) are acceptable ways to limit damage. The trouble is that they look awful. One alternative is the use of biological controls. In this case the controlling predator is a certain microscopic worm (nematode) which lays its eggs inside the larvae of the carrot fly. Horrific, but effective and chemical-free. The timing of application is vital as there must be carrot fly larvae in evidence to sustain the population of the predator, but when applied correctly the problem is quickly solved. The process begins earlier in the season when the hatching larvae

LEFT *Of all the root crops, carrots would be the easiest to grow were it not for the dreaded carrot fly. They played a huge part in the kitchens of a large house and no stockpot was complete without a carrot. They do not hold a place in the front rank today, but we grow a full Victorian range of seasonal varieties nonetheless.*

ABOVE *Grainne Piper considers which Scarlet Emperor runner bean to pick next under the gaze of the big yew and its companion, one of the original chusan palms (Trachycarpus fortunei), which stand outside the northern border of the Vegetable Garden.*
RIGHT *A late summer cobweb on a row of hazel sticks which are used to support peas. A fertile soil supports myriad insect life.*

are confused by the application of garlic granules; it is believed that this strange, low-flying insect is attracted by smell rather than sight. The garlic effectively prevents those larvae that have pupated in the soil and are hatching out from finding the carrots. Simple but ingenious.

This ongoing spectacle of work in progress is a great draw for the public's attention, as is the realisation that the work carried out in the garden, its successes and its failures (including plenty caused by the carrot fly), are the result of deliberate and diligent effort. The connection is then made that this is how it has been done for centuries, and it all begins to fall into place. It is, however, a fine balance to try and keep the enormous amount of visitors that we have happy, while at the same time keeping the garden as magical as it has always been. Heligan was once a place where people expected to creep through undergrowth and get mud on their boots. Now we are faced with having to keep overhanging branches cut back rigidly so the visitor does not get a twig in the eye or a soaking from dripping foliage. We need a great many visitors to balance the books and they all have to be catered for in the best possible way, which often means taking the time to stop and explain what we do.

Productive walled gardens represent a large slice of our heritage, and most of the visitors understand this, especially those of a certain age; what is not understood is how the work gets done, how a restoration like Heligan gets under way and is sustained. This is what I find myself explaining over and over again. I also often explain that we represent what happened all over the country in the mid nineteenth century and earlier. Every rectory, small manor house, large estate, castle and palace had walled gardens to produce food. It was standard practice amongst the moneyed classes: imports were minimal, labour was cheap and skills were high, as prior to the Industrial Revolution much of England's economy was land based.

My own family were classic exponents of this Industrial Revolution 'boom and build' practice. They were good, honest burghers of St Austell, solid middle-class types, doctors and lawyers, who holidayed every summer in the north-east of England. One year in the early nineteenth century they came across iron ore on their holiday, and in true Cornish fashion (everyone in Cornwall has mining blood in them somewhere along the line), they sunk a mine. With the proceeds they took on the leasehold of Porthpean House, which was then a pretty Georgian inn called The Dolphin, added two Victorian wings, and built two walled gardens. Within them they put up a heated stove house, a heated vinery, two peach houses and all the relevant support houses. The outskirts of St Austell are lined with houses built by merchants who made money out of china clay, tin mining or the like in the early to mid nineteenth century. They have large gardens and are screened from the St Austell to Truro road by huge banks of rhododendrons, Cornish Reds amongst them, which provided privacy and shelter. Most of the gardens behind the houses are walled in, with stables standing by for the production of manure. That was the way it was done in those days, that was what you did with your money, you put it into your place; this is how the conversation will often go before I sink to my knees again and carry on thinning the carrots.

Carrots were obviously an important crop, providing essential vitamin A and some colour at a time when it was not a great feature at the table. My father is fond of recounting the story

of Hetty, his great aunt's cook at Trebah (a beautiful garden on the Helford River) who only had two dinners in her repertoire: a brown one and a white one. The brown one consisted of brown Windsor soup (made from Windsor broad beans which we grow at Heligan), followed by some kind of brown fish like mackerel, then beef stew and rhubarb crumble for pudding. The white one may have included potato soup, plaice, chicken and vanilla ice cream. Parsnips, because they are deep-rooted, provided minerals such as phosphorous and iron and were also a valuable source of sugar. Surplus parsnips were fed to the horses for that very reason. They are a favourite with the tea room kitchens, where they are made into delicious winter soups and used as the trimmings for the hot gravy dinners. The lesser-known roots such as salsify and scorzonera also take up some room and are worth mentioning. Salsify, which looks and grows like a smaller, hairier parsnip, came from Russia as long ago as the sixteenth century, and is delicious roasted. Scorzonera is a thin black root which is also at its best when roasted. Hamburg parsley is grown for its white root, which makes the white sauce to accompany hot ham; it is something rarely seen outside Germany these days. Beetroot also features in the root section, as do turnips and winter radishes which, despite being brassicas, fit in here because their manner of growing is that of a root.

## Legumes: The Nitrogen Boost

Whilst all six courses of the rotation are vital for the building of soil fertility and the breakup of the cycles of pests and diseases, there is no greater contributor to the soil than the legume family which, for our purposes, is made up of peas and beans. No one can satisfactorily explain the mystery of the means by which the leguminous plant takes atmospheric nitrogen, holds it in bacteria which live on nodules attached to its roots, and releases the same nitrogen to nourish itself and other plants when it dies or is cut down. Runner beans, broad beans, peas, French beans and soya beans all do this, and they are vital. Apart from attention from slugs, runners, broads and French beans present few problems in their cultivation, and indeed runner beans are one of the few annual crops that can grow in the same place year after year.

Peas, however, are in the same league as brassicas when it comes to crop protection. No sooner does a young pea germinate and nose up through the ground to the daylight than it becomes very vulnerable to attack from the sky: the woodpigeon again. The sweet tips of young peas are a delicacy for the woodpigeon, so the netting of the crop must begin at the pre-emergent stage. Prior to this, the young plants have hazel or beech twigs implanted next to them so their first tendrils have something to cling on to. The coppicing of hazel for the production of twigs and poles for the very purpose of supporting peas and other plants in the garden would have been common practice throughout the Victorian era, and it is something we are returning to now as the woodland throughout the estate is reintegrated. Each year the requirement for pea sticks for the pea crop alone is somewhere in the region of three hundred, and all must be cut to a height of six feet and have a similar spread. Once the young peas are growing through their twigs, the larger pea sticks have to be carefully driven into the ground

LEFT *The onions have been recently eased out of the ground, the soil shaken off their roots, and the bulbs with foliage still attached laid out on the soil surface to harden off. This view is from north to south; the chimneys of Heligan House are just visible in the distance.* BELOW LEFT *'Plant on the shortest day and lift on the longest day' goes the old saying about shallots. The gourmet selection of the allium family, they have a subtler flavour than any onion.*

so the plants can cling on to them. Pea rows of around one hundred feet in length and over six feet in height do not stand alone; a gale of wind from the east would flatten even the great hedges, and so the peas have to be supported again by a system of posts and wires. Clive has become an expert at moving quietly up and down the rows, tying in the pea sticks to the wires with jute twine. It is a long and painstaking task, but a necessary one. As the peas begin to swell, so the pigeons begin to take renewed interest, and we have to scare them off by all available means – this can include the shotgun, when measures are desperate. What with the normal problems associated with peas – such as mildew, pea moth and thrips (thunder flies) – also presenting themselves year after year, the successful cultivation of the pea crop becomes an enormous responsibility. We need them to demonstrate the typical varieties that were grown at the time, and our hedges of Champion of England, Magnum Bonum and Veitch's Western Express are truly magnificent. It is worth imagining just how many had to be grown, picked, shucked and cooked to feed a full household in the Victorian era; it is quite an achievement to be able to reproduce this feat today.

## Onions

This is a huge family, of which we grow a number of varieties: onions, shallots, garlic, spring onions, tree onions, Welsh onions, chives and leeks. The onion collection has grown over the years to include varieties rarely seen beyond the show bench, such as Reliance and Southport Red Globe. Just as with all our crops they are grown for use in the tea room's kitchen, and just as in Victorian times most of them are grown from seed.

It warms the heart to see the young plants riffling in the breeze in the early summer, but it takes a great deal of effort to get them there. The crop is raised in 108 cell modules, 3 seeds per cell. When two inches high they are thinned to one plant per cell. Then, when large enough to be eased out of their cells at the end of April, they are planted out at six inches apart in the row. Six 100-foot rows equals 1200 onion plants. This careful operation is almost always carried out by Kathy and her helper Grainne Piper, from walking boards, which are in effect long pieces of skirting board that we lay over the damp ground in order to stop our big boots and heavy bodies from compacting the soil and preventing it from breathing. The shallots are a great deal simpler: they should be planted on the shortest day and lifted on the longest day, with no further complications. A suitably sized bulb is selected from the previous season's crop and pushed gently into the soil. In no time they are pushing their sturdy green claws skyward and by midsummer the first of the new season's allium crop is ready. Garlic requires a little more patience. It really belongs in the Mediterranean and needs warmer outdoor weather than we can provide. However, if sown in pots in autumn, and kept in a cold frame for the winter before being planted out in February, it can produce an adequate crop.

There are no such difficulties to be had with leeks, which are a very important staple crop. They start life in an open ground seedbed before being transplanted to their final resting place. They sit quite happily from midsummer right through until the following spring, and are dug

as required. The winter crop is preceded by a crop of summer leeks which, from a February sowing indoors in boxes, comes to fruition towards the end of the summer, the shanks being slightly more tender and juicy than the slower growing, more ponderous fat leeks of winter. Spring onions are sown in succession throughout the summer and our new arrival, the perennial tree onion, is creating interest because it produces tiny, perfectly formed onion bulbs, three-quarters of the way up its stem.

## Pumpkins

The pumpkins, squashes, gourds, courgettes and marrows have taken on something of a celebrity status over the last few years. The range is enormous; it starts with the tiny varieties Sweet Dumpling and Baby Bear and ends with the massive Atlantic Giant, which takes two men to lift. In between are extraordinary curly ones like Tromboncino, double headers such as Turk's Turban and peculiar coloured pumpkins like Blue Hubbard, which is a strange translucent grey. Once planted at the end of May or beginning of June they are allowed to romp away at their own pace and in their own style. It would be impossible to go wandering in between the plants to check them or pull weeds, because most varieties are trailing and send their shoots far afield, intermingling with their neighbours as they grow. It is quite a sight, and the mass of foliage makes for a good weed suppressant in itself.

As the growing season nears its end, the crops in what we call the miscellaneous, or 'bits and pieces' section, the sixth and final course of the rotation, reach their peak. By October the leaf beets, that is, perpetual spinach and various different coloured chards, are in their prime. In the nitrogen-rich soil of the Vegetable Garden the plants reach a phenomenal size. This is partly because we only crop them according to the needs of the kitchen. The celery that has lain all season in its trench is tied up with brown paper, to blanch its hearts to a sweet creamy white (blanching is the exclusion of light, which allows the plant to continue growing, but gives it a paler colour – resulting in a much sweeter taste); and its rooting relation, celeriac, is balling up well. The French beans, grown for their dried seed, are now being picked. They are laid on the wide slate slabs of the Melon House, where they are dried and hulled, after which they are stored in Kilner jars – just as they would have been in the larder next to the kitchens in Heligan House.

## Perennials

For many, the delights of an old-fashioned kitchen garden lie with the perennial crops, the primary two being asparagus and globe artichokes. They are the subject of continual interrogation from visitors at any time of year, and although both have been in cultivation in England for centuries, they were probably only known to the initiated few until around a hundred years ago, being costly both to produce and to buy.

The asparagus beds are heaped up a good foot above normal soil level and are bare from November to April. They bear a strong resemblance to long, freshly dug mass graves. From

the end of April to the third week of June they produce their tips or spears, which look, from a distance, like lots of green twigs stuck into the soil. From then on the cutting stops and the crop is allowed to continue growing in order to take the nourishment from its foliage back down into the deep-rooting crown, from where the tips originate. The huge mass of green, feathery foliage that appears from the opening tips waves in the wind and reaches five or six feet in height. Every morning, as the weather turns colder, the foliage becomes covered in heavy autumn dew and a mass of tiny spider webs.

Globe artichokes, and their more ornamental cousins the cardoons, also invite plenty of queries. Although they were known to and cultivated by the Romans, as was asparagus, they look very unusual. It is not until those that remain uncropped produce their enormous blue flowers that people realise they are nothing more than huge thistles, albeit tasty ones. It is impossible to miss this plant: long stems with green tennis balls on the end, shooting

ABOVE *The secret with asparagus is to cut it while it is small. When the whole spear is edible as these are, the taste experience reaches a new level. Although there are two 100-foot long beds in full production, not much of the crop makes it to the tea room!*

out from a large clump of jagged foliage. The flowering lasts throughout the summer and is a welcome addition to the garden.

Everything we grow has been cultivated since Victorian times, but fashions come and go in both the garden and the kitchen. Sea kale is a good case in point. This member of the cabbage tribe, which grows wild on the pebbly beaches of Sussex and Kent, was introduced by the Romans, who rated it most highly. It is very sweet and succulent with a faint hint of cabbage when blanched. It was always grown in grand, old walled gardens where staff and time were plentiful, and it is now on the verge of a comeback, as chefs once again begin to recognise its value.

Rhubarb, of course, never fell out of favour, and our rhubarb patch is large and abundant, producing thin pink slips in the spring and chunky red branches all through the summer

RIGHT *The pink stems of forced sea kale are almost translucent. They have blanched beautifully under their pots as the spring temperatures pick up. Sadly the pink will disappear in the cooking.* FAR RIGHT *Not so with rhubarb, which has also been forced. The pink is heightened on cooking, and as the earliest fruit of the season rhubarb is always welcomed.* OPPOSITE PAGE *Forcing pots for rhubarb and sea kale. Begged, stolen, borrowed, bought and donated from all over the country, the tall ones are for rhubarb, the stubby ones for sea kale.*

months. The best we have is Hawke's Champagne. Buy yourself a crown or two of it, just for a treat – it far outstrips Timperley Early for flavour.

The perennial crops do not move, and as such they are a blessing to the backs of the gardeners. The asparagus plants need some earthing up each year, and along with the globe artichokes they also benefit from a good mulch of seaweed. There is no double digging involved, however. This is the exhausting task that is fundamental to the maintenance of our soil. It is phenomenally hard work, made doubly so by the incorporation of horse manure in the bottom of the empty trench.

With our six-course rotation firmly in place, the Vegetable Garden is double dug with manure incorporated every third year, before the potato crop and before the cucurbits. The operation is carried out with what we know as a Cornish shovel, a long-handled tool with an arrow-shaped head, the tool of choice in most Celtic parts of the world, be it

Cornwall, Scotland or Ireland. It saves the back as the shoulder, arm and stomach muscles do all the work. The great winter dig can begin as early as August when the ground is cleared of the summer's crops. This is a long and tiring task and is entirely weather dependent, since rain can stop play at any given moment. I wish that all of our visitors could see this extraordinary feat being carried out, so integral is it to our project. Not only does it revive memories of agriculture and gardening as they were in Victorian times; it serves to reinforce the knowledge that, as I keep saying, it all begins with the soil.

## Bulbs

As if all these vegetables were not enough, the Vegetable Garden is also home to a substantial collection of spring and summer flower bulbs, the whimsy of our Horticultural Director Philip McMillan Browse. When Philip was but a boy, his father took up the post of headmaster at the school on St Mary's in the Isles of Scilly, and Philip's holidays were spent packing daffodils and gladioli, and grading potatoes.

This fondness for the early flower bulb crops – always such a significant part of the Cornish and Scillonian horticultural industry – has never left him. He recounts a typically vivid story

of the very first day he and his family arrived on Scilly, and how they were taken to the Atlantic Hotel on St Mary's for lunch. In the middle of the table there sat a huge vase of brightly coloured flowers. On enquiring of the waitress what they were, Philip's mother received the reply in a strong Scillonian accent: 'Them's ixias.' We still grow ixias and plenty of species gladioli that were around in Victorian times, along with *Brodiaea laxa*, *Camassia esculenta* and *Iris bucharica*. Visitors bombard us with queries as to why we grow flowers in the Vegetable Garden; the answer is that it brightens up a garden which for much of the season lies under a sea of green. The beds to the side of the path running from north to south through the Vegetable Garden also hold flowers, and these sweet Williams, wallflowers, asters and antirrhinums would originally have been used for cutting as well as scent and display.

## Fruit

No kitchen garden can live up to its name without substantial quantities of fruit, and the emphasis on fruit in Victorian times was enormous. Imports were few, and only large estates were able to produce their own oranges, bananas and pineapples. Apples, pears, plums and soft fruits were grown as a matter of course. As with vegetables, there were hundreds of different varieties of every type of fruit imaginable, and the good ones have survived to be grown again. Some, like gooseberries, are still the subject of specialist horticultural shows in the north of England, and take up nearly half our fruit cage, grown as both bushes and single-stemmed cordon trained plants. There are red-, white- and blackcurrants and a handful of ancient, long-forgotten raspberry varieties like Norfolk Giant and Cornish White. Our strawberry variety, Royal Sovereign – always the best strawberry in terms of flavour, with its paper-thin skin and sweet white flesh – does not make it into the fruit cage. This crop has to be rotated around the garden, whereas the berry fruits remain in position for up to ten years and beyond.

Nothing gives more pleasure at Heligan than the sight of the apple tunnel in the spring, covered in blossom from top to bottom. Encompassing a typical range of varieties which would have been prominent in the Victorian era, it has been planted according to the time of flowering. The trees at the top end by Flora's Green flower first and the rest follow in descending order, with the late-flowering varieties sited at the bottom so as to avoid damage from frost (cold air drains downhill).

In the course of any late summer day it is a common event to get stuck behind a group of people in the narrow lanes of the garden. The apple tunnel is a particularly bad place for traffic. It was along the tunnel I was walking one day when I got stuck behind an old-timer and his wife, who were genuinely crawling along. Finally they ground to a halt by the apple known as Lord Derby. It was then that the old boy mumbled through an ill-fitting pair of false teeth in a strong cockney accent: 'Ah yes, the Kent 'oppin apple.' I could not for the life of me work out what he meant, and was left thinking about folk dancing – that was enough for me to beg his forgiveness and ask for a translation. It turned out that Lord Derby ripened and was eaten at the same time as the hop crop in Kent and had thus acquired the

name; a curious fact, seeing that Lord Derby is today thought of mostly as a cooking apple,
but it is in fact dual purpose, both cooker and eater. On a slightly different note, I got stuck
another time by Lord Derby behind two elderly ladies from the North of England, one of
whom exclaimed in knowing terms and a very thick Yorkshire accent: 'Eeh, Lord Derby! Yer
can always tell a Lord Derby by the great big bum on it.' Indeed Lord Derby does have two
ridges that resemble the human backside.

The apple arch is home to a wide range of varieties. As well as the much commented upon
Lord Derby, there are other luminaries such as the Reverend W. Wilks, Arthur Turner and
Charles Ross in the tunnel. There are both 'cookers' and 'eaters' amongst them, and what
a sight they make when in full blossom, stark against the acid-green young leaves of the box
hedging which is planted beneath them.

## The Melon Yard

Like most gardens attached to large estates, Heligan was blessed with good walls. High, for
security and shelter, and thick, to support fruit trees and other ornamentals. We know there
were apples in the Vegetable Garden, but there is scant evidence of an orchard anywhere at

Heligan in the nineteenth century. Without any obvious orchard to restore, it fell upon us to utilise the walls to maximum effect: apples, pears and the stone fruits, plums, greengages, cherries and apricots, have all flourished (peaches were confined to the Peach House).

Growing trained fruit on walls is the horticultural equivalent of high art. It requires understanding and patience, a keen eye and a deft pair of hands. The stunning curved wall that divides the Melon Yard from the Vegetable Garden is pockmarked with a million holes where fruit was 'nailed and tagged' over the centuries. Before wire came to be used in the latter years of the nineteenth century, every single branch had be tied to a nail with cloth. Now the years of neglect are being rolled back and the walls are once again covered with pears, cherries, apricots and apples, some trained by the oblique cordon method, which is a single-stemmed tree offset at an angle of forty-five degrees. These old fruit production skills are being lost in this country, and the knowledge required to produce table-ripe fruit is also vanishing. Sadly, head gardeners did not keep journals documenting their methods. They ought to have done; woolly peaches and hard pears were not looked upon kindly by those paying the wages, and head gardeners had to have their wits about them. It was left to a handful of writers such as Loudon, McIntosh and those who contributed to the various gardeners' journals of the time to record this for posterity, but unfortunately their accuracy is questionable, and they often disregarded geographical variations.

Despite the decline in specialist skills and other vagaries involved in our restoration, such as climatic conditions, a well-grown fan-trained plum on a wall, such as we grow, is precisely the type of sight one would have expected to see in a Victorian garden. The same, however, cannot be said of a ripe pineapple. The Melon Yard is a pretty yard with a run of three cold frames and various buildings which include a Potting Shed, a Tool Shed, a long lean-to, and a two-storied building with a forcing room and a fruit storage room. The Melon Yard has been referred to as the engine room of the garden; this is where the propagating and growing of all our seed-raised plants is carried out. As its centrepiece it has the Melon House, a fine early nineteenth-century glasshouse, in which we grow cucumbers and melons. Beneath it is the Pineapple Pit.

This triumph of Victorian engineering and horticulture is once again in full production, and has proved an endless source of fascination for staff and visitors alike. There is plenty of

documentary evidence on growing pineapples as a crop in the nineteenth century, and in reality it was probably no more unusual than growing, say, orchids. Although quite a testing task requiring specific climatic conditions, the Victorian gardeners soon grasped what was required and set about producing quantities of good, edible fruits for their masters and for the show bench. There were designated classes for pineapples at horticultural shows throughout the country. So when a consignment of unrooted tops and sideshoots appeared at Easter in 1995, Philip and I managed to root them successfully in our Victorian pit. The offspring of the same stock are still flowering and fruiting in their twelve-inch terracotta pots in the pit today.

Just as in the Victorian era, the successful production of pineapples is governed by correct management of heat, produced by horse manure situated to the front and back of the growing chamber. The heat travels through the honeycomb brickwork that divides manure pit from growing chamber and then into the chamber itself, where it rises and causes condensation to collect on the underside of the glass frames. Dry heat is what members of the bromeliad family prefer, and so moisture levels have to be carefully controlled by ventilation, even in winter. Bromeliads need to be watered through the centre of the plant as well as at the roots, but it is fatal if moisture collects in the centre and is not used up in the winter, when the plants are not growing as strongly as in the summer. This results in rotting and death. Just as with citrus, the most common cause of poor results with pineapples is over-watering.

There are four other cold frames in the Melon Yard, each of which has an important role to play. There is a run of three, the lowest of which is the 'hardening off' frame, where all the plants for the Vegetable Garden acclimatise before being planted out. The two frames above are rotated between Royal Sovereign strawberries in one and cucumbers and melons in the other. Distinctly different from their culture in the Melon House, in this frame the ridge cucumbers and melons are allowed to sprawl over the soil without interference.

The fourth frame, which is found directly beneath the Pineapple Pit, is a forcing frame. This became evident during the restoration when, after the years of accumulated debris had been removed, its floor was found to be made up of clinker (which is the hard remains from the coal furnaces on steam trains). As recently as last year we began using this frame to 'force'

ABOVE *Mike and I turn fresh manure for the Pineapple Pit. The heap is turned three times within a fortnight before being introduced into the manure beds to the front and rear of the growing chamber. The turning heats the heap evenly.*
ABOVE RIGHT *The line of three cold frames in the Melon Yard. Beyond them, the two-storeyed building that houses fruit on its top floor, with the forcing room below*

asparagus, that is, to grow it out of season, by the use of a hot bed. Hotbedding would have been commonplace in Victorian times and we felt duty bound to bring the practice back. Just as many people today demand strawberries at Christmas, so the Victorians wanted new potatoes by Easter and rhubarb well before the season had started. They grew it themselves, however, being unable to rely on jet travel for the provision of such exotics.

In the case of asparagus, supplies of raw materials were of the utmost importance. The manure that provided the heat which gave the practice of hotbedding its name was always available, as large stables were kept at Heligan and horses used for travel, work and sport. The idea behind hotbedding is simple: a large pile of fermenting horse manure is covered with a thin layer of soil, and seeds or plants are grown in this warm soil with glass frames or 'lights' on top. This encourages growth at a very fast rate and produces extraordinary results.

Seeds take a couple of days to germinate, and softwood cuttings will root in no time. At the beginning of the 2003 season we decided to move one of our two asparagus beds to a new position, directly below the original one in the Vegetable Garden. In the process of lifting the huge, matted, octopus-like crowns it became evident that they needed to be divided. So the new bed was planted, with plenty left over to fill both a hot bed and a holding bed for crops to be forced in years to come (once you have forced an asparagus crown, it either needs several years to recover in a bed, or it should be simply discarded and composted). With regular supplies of fresh horse manure coming in for use in the Pineapple Pit, and being dumped directly beneath the frame, there was no harm in

RIGHT *Smooth Cayenne pineapples begin to ripen as the hot summer wears on. These plants have descended from the original stock that Philip McMillan Browse and I planted on the first Bank Holiday Monday in May 1994.* OPPOSITE PAGE *A Blenheim Orange melon swings happily in its handmade melon net in the Melon House. It is one of the most challenging of all fruits to grow, in my opinion, much harder even than the pineapple.*

stealing some for the hotbed. And grow the asparagus we did throughout March, cropping at least a month before the maincrop came in. Old Squire Tremayne would have been proud of us.

## The Potting Shed

For some years now the Melon Yard has felt like it belongs to our generation of gardeners. This was not always the case. In the early days of restoration, as stories unfolded and the garden and soil gave up their secrets, the sense of the past was enormously strong. Sometimes joyous and often melancholy, there were and still are days when one could almost smell the past and the people that inhabited the garden. The lives of those who worked the land one hundred and fifty years ago were hard, living conditions poor and wages meagre – not as hard as those who mined tin or china clay for a living, but hard enough all the same. Up with the dawn, a full day's work and then a long walk home to more chores, such as fetching in wood or drawing water from a well or pump. Although the Melon Yard has been entirely rebuilt from ruins (there were around seventy large, self-sown ash and sycamore trees growing in it at the time of rediscovery), the connection with those who worked this frame yard and used the buildings is at times very strong indeed.

ABOVE *The collection of old tools has grown over the years, mainly through kind donations. It is amazing what people have collected. Hedging shears and brass sprayers are here joined by an asparagus knife (front left).* OPPOSITE PAGE *Beki Marriott and Jeremy Pedersen clean tools before hanging them up in the Potting Shed; a time-honoured tradition, worthy of any serious gardener.*

There is no doubt that what we call the Potting Shed has been 'the real thing' since John Nelson rebuilt it in 1993. So intent was he on accuracy that he decided to use lime as opposed to cement when putting the slates on the roof. This, of course, was quite the correct thing to do, but he chose to do it on a day with just a little too much rain, and the lime mix never set properly. The result was a leaky Potting Shed. But despite the drips the Potting Shed quickly became our headquarters where we discussed everything, kept everything and ducked out of everyone's way. Compost was stacked under the bench, along with loam, sand and peat for making potting mixes. There were shelves of terracotta pots donated from an always generous public, and all our tools hung on the walls, cleaned at the end of each day in the stone trough by the Tool Shed. The Potting Shed soon took on the earthy smell that all potting sheds have: a mix of soil, tobacco, oil and damp wood. It never fails to intrigue people how sheds such as this still exist. Although visitors are allowed in, we put a bamboo cane across the door during very busy periods, or there is no room in which to move. They peer in and strike up a conversation about the potting shed they remember best, usually belonging to their granddad. It is fantastic.

Adjoining the Potting Shed is the Tool Shed, which has become a collection and display point for some fascinating pieces of equipment donated to the gardens over the years. Heart-shaped turfing irons, a Planet hoe which is still used in the Flower Garden, innumerable brass sprayers and some terrifying gin traps; they all give a fascinating insight into the types of tool used down through the years.

The Melon Yard is joined to the Italian Garden via a flight of two steps, through the old thunderbox room where the two lavatories, for use by the garden staff centuries ago, are sited

side by side. On the Melon Yard side is the six-foot deep pit where the night soil was composted before being returned to the garden. This room, in the north-west corner of the yard, has the names of gardeners still visible on the plaster. Many of the names are replicated on the war memorial in the nearby village of St Ewe, commemorating those gardeners who fell in the First World War. It is wonderful to see this graffiti from the olden days – obviously the head gardener never went into the thunderbox room. Above it is a ledge where the boy who stoked the Melon House boiler may have slept. Next door to it is what has simply become known as the two-storeyed building. Downstairs is a windowless cellar where Kathy grows mushrooms through the spring and early summer. Upstairs is the Fruit Room, where we store a variety of crops such as seed potatoes, shallots, onions, apples and pears.

Over the years people have remarked that this room in particular holds some strong energy connected with the past. Personally, I will never forget what happened there one spring evening in 1994. In those days John Nelson was almost invariably the last man out of the garden and he did most of the locking up. Depending on the time of year and how many visitors were left in the garden, whoever was left of the workforce would shut the doors of the Melon Yard and the Flower Garden, put rabbit guards in place, and so on. One evening the task fell to me. It was gloomy, the sort of evening that makes you want to hurry on home. I had closed the bottom gates of the yard, shut the Potting Shed and locked the Fruit Room, which had recently been home to all that season's seeds, but they had mysteriously gone missing, and I was taking no further chances. I was on my way to shut the gate through to the Vegetable Garden when I heard them, footsteps in the Fruit Room. Impossible – I had just locked it – but I knew the sound of footfalls on those bare boards and I absolutely knew there was nowhere for anyone to hide up there. The hairs stood up on the back of my neck but I knew I had to go and check just in case someone...no, this was crazy, but there was nothing for it, I had to go back. With my heart in my mouth I climbed the stairs and slowly turned the key in the lock and then the handle of the door. There was nobody there and I

RIGHT *Looking from the left, the second and third windows are those of the Potting Shed, which used to be our headquarters, and from where we could easily check on the comings and goings through the busy Melon Yard.*

went quickly on my way. The next day the box of seeds was back in the Fruit Room from where it had gone missing. I wish I could explain it but I can't; all I know is that the Melon Yard is a place with a history.

## The Flower Garden

The spring and summer seasons of 1994 saw the establishment of the Vegetable Garden and Melon Yard as working gardens. The focus then moved to the Flower Garden, and all through the winter of 1994/5 we worked on it as though our lives depended upon it. In the autumn extra hands were brought in on 'back to work' schemes. We looked like forced labour at the gulags as we worked in gangs, forming long lines across the garden, which had just been ploughed and now needed picking over in minute detail to remove the trash and perennial weeds. We forked over the earth in the coldest winter any of us could remember in a long time. The ground froze over the Christmas period and I can remember us trying to work in

the permafrosted soil, eventually having to give up in the face of futility. When the thaw came we slunk back to work with a certain sense of foreboding; the spring seemed a long way ahead. This was the time when no one quite knew if there was any money to keep the ship afloat, and when there nevertheless remained a sense that somehow the project would simply continue, and that the restoration would eventually reach some sort of completion – whatever that meant.

But we were broke and we knew it; and when a Christmas card appeared for everyone with a nice, pretty picture of a broken-down glasshouse, that was enough. I went to see Tim and told him, in the nicest possible way, that the troops were not interested in pretty cards – put twenty quid in them and you might make some friends. The message got through but it was a long, hard winter, despite the presence of a TV production company in the autumn making a half-hour documentary on the restoration. Our hopes were kept up by the thought that the Flower Garden would complete our productive gardens. The Vegetable Garden and the Melon Yard were already functioning at full capacity; now all that was needed was the rightful place for the cut flowers to be grown and the remains of the glasshouses to be finished and put in working order.

Before any of that could get underway, there was another massive clearing job to do. It is astonishing how much rubbish can accumulate in old walled gardens. Although the Flower Garden had been used as a garden by the Thomas family, who had leased Heligan House before it was converted into flats, all the hallmarks of gradual abandonment and slow decline were evident: broken panes of glass, endless roofing slates, wire, bits of guttering and pipe, and not much of any use. Except, that is, for the most important thing of all: there was enough left of the three major glasshouses for John Nelson to get templates from which to rebuild them. It is still not entirely clear what the full range of Flower Garden glasshouses encompassed, but today we have a Peach House, a double Vinery and a fruit house (which we call the Citrus House because it houses our citrus collection during the winter months). By the spring of 1995 enough progress had been made, and before we knew it the Flower Garden was ready for planting.

The Flower Garden is a curious little walled garden, on account of its peculiar rhomboid shape alone. It is ringed on the north and east sides by glasshouses, and has a dipping pool for filling water carriers in the middle and sloping beds on either side. The dipping pool is an unusual eighteenth-century feature in itself, put in before running water became standard. The garden is also unique given that the ground beneath the Peach House that faces south-west is on a significant slope, and as such is the first ground to warm up in the spring. There can be no doubt that this was specifically designed and

BELOW *The Flower Garden sweeping up to the Peach House, with the foliage of the peaches clearly visible inside against the white of the limewashed walls. The last remaining fig, to the right of the brick chimney, would once have been grown in a glasshouse.*

laid out to grow the earliest crops of the season, combining a perfect slope with excellent drainage and good access to water – although the dipping pool has never been filled by accident, nor by means of natural drainage. At the turn of the nineteenth century, the Somerset firm of Green and Carter had installed a system of pipes and ram pumps to move water around the estate. With this system now fully restored, the water from a spring in an adjoining valley about a mile to the west is pumped back up to a reservoir at the top of the gardens, which is capable of holding forty thousand gallons. The water is then gravity-fed to stand pipes around the gardens and is used as required. It also fills the dipping pool.

Because the water and the glass of the greenhouses reflect a massive amount of heat, and the brick walls soak it up only to release it later, this garden can get extremely hot

during the summer months. Put a few hundred visitors in it and the temperature rises further. There is not as much room as there is in the Vegetable Garden, so it can also become quite congested on a busy day. John Nelson sensibly built a brick terrace in front of the Vineries and Citrus House to ease the pressure. However this may prove to be to the detriment of the vines themselves, for the terrace is covering what would have been their bread basket, an enormous manure-filled bed into which they spread their roots and fed sumptuously. For these Vineries we have a giant of nineteenth-century horticulture to thank. Sir Joseph Paxton, MP, packed a lot into his life; as well as being head gardener to the Duke of Devonshire at Chatsworth in Derbyshire, he designed and built the Crystal Palace. On a smaller but much more significant scale (for horticultural purposes) he designed the first flatpack glasshouse. Careful inspection

ABOVE *Of all the cool glasshouse late-season dessert grapes, Lady Hutt produces the biggest bunches by far. Other varieties include Chasselas Rose, Muscat of Hamburgh, Mrs Pearson and Gros Colmar*

of the Vineries in the Flower Garden show that they are made up of sections, and whilst this may not seem like rocket science today, it was a stroke of genius in 1850 and revolutionised the market place for glasshouses. Even then magazines and papers were full of 'special offers' and 'amazing knockdown prices', and Paxton's idea was swept up. It was fortunate that such glasshouses found their way to Cornwall – but then the Tremaynes had been at the forefront of horticultural developments for some time, a fact to which the Vineries are testament. Before Paxton and his flatpack idea, and before solid fuel boilers pushed hot water through cast-iron pipes, the Vineries had been heated by fires lit in the hollow walls. In some ways Cornwall was very much up to the minute with progress.

Dessert grapes can be temperamental. Their glasshouse is heated in order to start them off early and finish them off at the end of the season, thereby avoiding the fungal problems brought about by cooler night temperatures. They are not heated now because the boiler next to the Head Gardener's Office is still defunct. However they do finish well and we have had some fantastic crops over the years, but this is dependent upon the bunches being thinned properly and a careful eye kept out for any signs of grey mould (Botrytis). Varietal choice is important too. The early season varieties such as Chasselas Rose sweeten well, as do the mid season Muscat of Hamburghs, but the later varieties such as Mrs Pearson and Gros Colmar sometimes have difficulty in attaining that real sweetness which you look for in grapes.

Gardening becomes such an enormous pleasure with these grand old greenhouses at one's disposal. The arctic mornings, when fingers freeze from picking sprouts and backs can barely straighten up to lean against the shovel, seem miles away when one stares at the perfect bloom on a ripening bunch of Muscat of Hamburgh grapes. All possible space in the Vineries is used

to hold summer-flowering bulbs in pots, such as *Tigridia*, *Polianthes* and the much commented on spider lily *Hymenocallis*. A substantial collection of nerines grow here too, including the extra-special *N. flexuosa* 'Alba', which has a coating of diamond dust all over its petals, making them look as though someone had showered them with fairy icing sugar.

We have had our disasters over the years. In 2002 our vines, after eight happy seasons of growth and many bunches of delicious grapes, decided to curl their toes up and set about dying. There was a lot of head-scratching and chin-rubbing and consulting of experts and sending away of material, and finally a conclusion was reached: they had died of a little-known fungal disease called Eutypa which was known to attack glasshouse vines. There was nothing for it but to dig them out and start again, but to satisfy ourselves that the incoming plants were given optimum conditions, we would have to remove the soil that they had been grown in – which might be harbouring the fungus – and replace it with new. Everything went quiet and eyes were averted: who was going to carry out this monumental task?

That autumn's newest recruit, top international speedway rider and Argentinian champion, Emiliano Sanchez, had already proved himself adept at double digging in the Vegetable Garden. He grabbed his shovel and said: 'Leave this to me'. The nature of a place like Heligan means that every now and then it throws up an absolute gem, and Emiliano is one such. The greatest heroes in the garden are the foot-soldiers who slog and slog through every winter with shovel in one hand and barrow of muck in the other. Within two weeks Emiliano had dug out to shoulder level the worst soil imaginable – it was a miracle that the vines had survived in

LEFT *The notice board keeps visitors up to date with important goings-on in the garden.* OPPOSITE PAGE *The area in front of the Vineries would almost certainly have been soil beds. The vines were planted outside the glasshouse, fed through holes in the walls and trained up inside, parallel to the glass. Today, small beds hold* Amaryllis belladonna *and a large terrace accommodates visitors.*

there for so long. He then had to empty two of the Flower Garden compost heaps into the pit to bring the soil level to halfway, and then fill the rest up to ground level with surplus soil barrowed from the Vegetable Garden. It was a marathon effort and the new vines are now growing happily.

When the citrus trees are heaved on to the terrace for the duration of the summer their place is taken by an unusual collection of tomatoes, aubergines, chillies and peppers. These are grown in large terracotta pots by Sylvia Travers, a Dubliner who joined the staff after completing her studies at the Botanical Gardens at Glasnevin, in her home city in the Republic of Ireland. She is responsible for growing all the fruit in the productive gardens, and she combines this with producing the glasshouse crops, as well as the melons and the cucumbers. It is a responsible job requiring skill, patience and minute attention to detail. The third key player, who bears the weight of responsibility in the productive gardens alongside Sylvia and Kathy, is Andrea Murfitt. A skilful plantswoman from the West Midlands with a wry sense of humour and a great love of plants, Andrea has made the Flower Garden her own over the last few years. Although half the ground is devoted to early summer vegetables and annual and perennial herbs, the Flower Garden was designed to produce flowers for the house. It still fulfils this role today, with the flowers finding their way to the tea room tables, or decorating the Potting Shed bench or Head Gardener's Office. That said, most of the bloom remains uncut in the row for the enjoyment of the public; only so many armfuls of *Godetia*, *Clarkia* and *Cleome* can be picked within the limits of practicality. This is a garden in which to breathe in the heady scent of nectar, to close your eyes and listen to the bees buzzing amongst the long rows of flowers: *Scabiosa*, *Helenium*, *Coreopsis*, *Echinacea* and *Rudbeckia*. There are species lilies and *Eremurus*, the giant foxtail lily. There are *Magnolia grandiflora* trained on one north-facing wall and *Camellia reticulata* 'Captain Rawes', trained on the other. There are beds full of fat cos lettuces, and curly endive tied up with string to blanch out the

hearts. There are purple French beans and rows of summer savory, there are figs on the fig tree, and looking down on these underlings from a great height is the triumphant Peach House, filled to the brim in July with ripe Duke of York and Rochester peaches. This garden is so abundant, it is a triumph of the restoration. Just as with the Vegetable Garden it is worked on a careful rotation, and all the produce finds its way to the tea room kitchens. Every morning throughout the summer Andrea moves between the beds of herbs, cutting parsley, chives and thyme and pulling bunching carrots or spring onions just as she might have done one hundred and fifty years ago. I can picture the scene quite clearly. She may have started a good deal earlier than our start time of eight o'clock and she would have, in all probability, been male, but not necessarily. On presenting the box of herbs to the scullery maid she would have nearly fainted at the smell of freshly baking pasties or bread that drifted out from the kitchens. Then she would have gone back to work.

Not much has changed, except that the produce now goes to the tea room instead. We respond to visitors who question the final destination of the produce with pride. Most seem to think that what we grow would feed armies. They shake their heads in disbelief on hearing the sad news that a few dozen cabbages will not make coleslaw for a thousand people, as is the requirement on busy days in the summer. However working our productive gardens as they would have been worked in times gone by, with no machinery other than a tractor to haul manure, but still maintaining maximum output, has been a fantastic experience for all those fortunate enough to be involved. We have learned a great deal about many different crops in a very short space of time. We have got to know which varieties we like, and which ones we don't, and all of us have come across things that we might otherwise never have heard of.

## The Head Gardener's Office

It is hard to guess what sort of a man a head gardener was in 1850. It would be easy to paint a picture of him as a stern disciplinarian with a Wackford Squeers way of treating the pot boys. In one picture of New Zealand in 1880, the head gardener is a small figure hiding among huge tree ferns, looking decidedly uneasy about the photographic session of which he is the subject. He has a wing collar on and a tiny bowler hat is perched on top of his head. In a slightly later group photograph of the staff, perhaps about 1905, a head gardener is difficult to pick out because there are too many senior-looking figures who appear much the same in both age and dress. In that photograph one young lad is seated, or rather slouched, his cap is at a jaunty angle, smoking a cigarette in a rather nonchalant manner. Perhaps it was the norm or maybe the head gardener was not that hard on the troops. It is difficult to imagine it happening today.

One of the iconic photographs of Heligan shows the rusty kettle hanging over the fireplace in the Head Gardener's Office – but this picture can do little more than indicate that the man was partial to a cup of tea, or needed boiling water to sterilise knives and secateurs for pruning.

His office is centrally situated behind the Flower Garden, backing on to the Citrus House, and is reached via the boiler house which contains a defunct Britannia boiler. This enormous work of engineering would have sent hot water around the pipes in the Vineries to help start the vines off in the spring and ripen the grapes in the autumn. From his office next door, the head gardener would have been able to make sure that whoever was supposed to be stoking the boiler, controlling the temperature of the Vineries, was doing their job.

Whatever his character, the head gardener's job was a hugely important one – perhaps second only to that of the butler – and he may have been responsible for twenty or more

gardeners. On account of that he would have very likely been highly skilled. His role as a teacher would have been crucial and he would have known and appreciated this fact, having gained his own education serving his apprenticeship in another garden, or maybe even the same one. But undoubtedly his most important job — and the one that took up most of his time — was the production of the highest quality produce for the house. And with growing came presentation: vegetables washed and bunched appropriately, peaches without bruises, grapes with the burr unblemished, flowers cut to the right length and then tied up with raffia, and pot plants taken in looking their best. It was an awesome responsibility and head gardeners had the ear of their bosses, if they were interested; in some cases they became friends, as Sir Joseph Paxton did with the Duke of Devonshire at Chatsworth in the nineteenth century.

Situated neatly behind the Head Gardener's Office, Pencalenick is the name given to a glasshouse that came from the property of the same name on the Fal estuary between Heligan and Truro. The house is now a school, but it had belonged at one time to the prolific Williams family who have substantial properties in Cornwall, Caerhays, Werrington, Scorrier and Burncoose, to name a few. The purpose of this greenhouse is to show the type of foliage plants that would have been grown in abundance to fill Heligan House in all its pomp. There was an entire Flower Garden to provide blooms, and the foliage had to come from somewhere. With the availability of plants from all over the world by the late nineteenth century and the expertise to grow them well in place, a greenhouse of this nature would have been a must for a garden such as Heligan. Today it is lush with an abundance of greenery and some flower, in the shape of ferns, bromeliads, and cycads and other palms.

## The Banana House

On his way from his office into the garden, the head gardener would go through the boiler room. There he would have been able to check the state of the Britannia boiler if he felt so inclined. On stepping through the door into the garden, the first thing he would have seen was the Banana House. It is not known what variety of banana was grown in the house but *Musa basjoo*, a species of banana introduced into this country from Japan, where it was grown for the fibre produced by its leaves rather than its fruits, was in cultivation in England by 1881. It might seem curious that a glasshouse built specifically to house a single banana plant should face due north. Tucked under the north-facing wall of the Flower Garden, the Banana

House stays all day in total shade. Although we may think of bananas as needing full sun in order to produce high quality fruit, they are tolerant of shade. In southern India they grow as part of mixed forest farming systems, sometimes in quite thick shade. At the end of the nineteenth century, when the big beech tree below the Italian Garden and the *Rhododendron falconeri* outside the Head Gardener's office were relative babies, the Banana House may have received some dappled westerly sunlight in the evenings. Certainly it was heated because the old cast-iron pipes are still there.

## The Bee-Boles

The Bee-Boles must have exuded something of an eerie quality as Tim Smit and John Nelson cut their way through the undergrowth in 1991. No doubt their intended purpose quickly became clear, but from a distance they could easily pass for mini catacombs or burial chambers, and can be a little unsettling. These curious hollows, built into the wall, were designed to hold wicker 'skeps', a form of early beehive. Making up part of the southern end of the Vegetable Garden wall and adjoining the Melon Garden wall, they were perfectly placed for the bees to carry out their pollinating duties on plants throughout the garden, specifically fruit trees. It was a perfect system. The production of honey and wax were both important aspects of any estate, and to have the bees situated within the garden would have been ideal.

So, just as we had set about restoring everything else, the Bee-Boles had their turn. A man was found who could make skeps, and swarms of bees were introduced into them. This worked well for a while – until a number of visitors were stung, and it became obvious that Health and Safety would not sanction the siting of bee skeps in such close proximity to the route of the visitors.

Despite the departure of the bee colonies from the Bee-Boles, however, the honey bee still has a crucial role to play in the gardens and on the estate. Pollination, particularly of fruit crops, is the very important task of the honey bees, so they remain in residence, now in hives sited in the south-east corner of Steward's Meadow. At half a mile from the apple arch in the Vegetable Garden this may seem like a formidable distance, but in favourable weather bees will easily travel for two miles in search of pollen. What they do not like, however, are cold, wet and, particularly, windy conditions, when flying is difficult and much energy is expended. The critical time that this might happen is early in the spring after a winter of hibernation, when the bee's energy is at its lowest, yet it must still search for food for the colony. Some fruit crops, such as gooseberries and pears, come into flower very early, even in February, and bee activity is essential for them at that time. As fine weather is often too much to ask of a Cornish February and pollination is too important to leave to chance, other arrangements have to be made, and to this end a nesting site for the Red Masonry bee has been found in a hole on the south-facing wall of the Melon Yard. This little bee is harmless to humans and is a prolific pollinator. All the good work carried

out by the honey bee as it pollinates all manner of garden plants really does produce some wonderful results – as 230lb of honey taken to the tea room this year will testify.

Health and Safety issues need to be at the basis of all the decisions that we make as a public attraction. I remember the surface of the Melon Yard suffered a fate similar to the Bee-Boles, early in the summer of 1995. During our excavations in the Melon Yard we had come across several patches of clinker, the hard leftovers from coal-fired boilers turned to ash. As it was a material well known for its use as surfacing in old productive gardens, we decided to try and locate some. The Bodmin Light Railway service was able to provide clinker, so Mike Rundle was dispatched with tractor and trailer. The clinker duly arrived and was spread, and we all stood back and admired what we believed to be an original flooring surface for the Melon Yard around 1860. It just so happened that the summer of 1995 was very dry, and visitors began to appear in droves. No matter how much we did with the hose, by 11.30 a.m. every day the yard was thick with a choking black dust, which settled on clothes, in hair, on plants and on newly painted glasshouses. Finally, enough was enough; all the clinker was raked up and carted away.

One of Heligan's strongest suits is its policy of showing the visitor as much as possible and giving information to go with it. In the pioneering days of the restoration there was a strong feeling running through the team that the visitor should not feel constrained. Endless signs proclaiming extreme danger and ordering the reader to keep well clear were not felt to be very encouraging, and we wanted to share our extraordinary journey with whoever wanted to come and join in. Though much harder today on account of rigorous Health and Safety requirements than ten years ago, it is still possible to gain access to some of the working areas that might more usually be designated out of bounds.

Although the glasshouses are labelled 'Staff Only' for obvious reasons – straying fingers and thumbs on semi-ripe peaches lead to spoiled fruit – the Reserve Garden and the Poultry Yard, two brick-built walled gardens backing on to the Flower Garden, still play vital roles in the propagation of plants for the garden and are very much open to the public. The Reserve Garden is home to a giant of Victorian horticulture, a cold frame built by Messrs Foster and Pearson around 1880. A long, low frame structure with hinged glass lights that are propped open by a complicated system of wrought-iron props, it is where many young plants for the Vegetable and Flower Gardens are grown and hardened off before being planted out.

The Poultry Yard, which adjoins it to the east, is still something of a mystery. On its north-facing wall there are the remains of a structure whose wall is still covered in layer upon layer of encrusted limewash, suggesting that it was a glasshouse of some description – perhaps used for propagation, given a certain amount of shade created by the northerly aspect. This alleged propagation house would have had added shade cast over it from one of the oldest ornamental trees left in the garden: the handkerchief tree. This weather-beaten old soldier stands, or rather crouches, in the far eastern corner of the Sundial Garden. It is a forlorn sight, ducking out of the way of the east wind, its crown almost completely removed by centuries of punishment; its pearly white bracts are so delicate that they evoke sympathy when encountered at head height, where the last of the good growth on this venerable old tree is to be found.

LEFT *Freesia corymbosa fills the Vineries with a sweet scent. There were a multitude of glasshouses to produce scented and exotic plants for the house in the nineteenth century. Nowadays we have to make do with only the Vineries.*

*When the restoration began the Jungle was as impenetrable as its very name suggests. Self-seeded trees were everywhere, just as in the Northern Gardens. The ponds were silted up and due to the steepness of the incline, clearance was very difficult.*

# *Wild*
# Heligan

LEFT *Three stalwarts of the low ground in the Jungle show their paces. The yellow skunk cabbage,* Lysichiton americanus, *has* Gunnera manicata *behind it and a venerable tree fern,* Dicksonia antarctica, *to the right. It is a truly extraordinary sight.* ABOVE *Dog daisies are now beginning to spread, as the light creeps back in to what had become a dense and impenetrable landscape.*

The first visit to the Jungle is unforgettable. To stand at the top pond and look down the treescape is to realise that something very unusual lies ahead. To look back at the house behind, in its imperious position at the head of the steeply sided valley, turns the mind to the creator of such a place: who was the vision behind it, who took the bold decision to make this garden, here where there was once simply a stream trickling through woodland and down to the sea? Let these thoughts take you along the winding path that strikes deep into the Jungle.

## The Jungle

My grandmother, Jeane Petherick, was not an especially passionate gardener, but she was a skilled photographer. Throughout her life she kept very detailed photographic records. The results of her endeavours found their way into leather-bound albums which have been looked after and subsequently indexed by my father. In the book with 'J. P. 1915–1917' on the spine, one of the first photographs is of her husband, my grandfather, standing on the deck of the SS *Olympic* just before the Devon Yeomanry, in which regiment he served as lieutenant, landed at Suvla Bay. There are pictures of the enormous four-funnelled *Olympic* taken from another ship, and next to it are two untitled photographs of far-reaching views over scrub-covered mountainsides, which must be the Dardanelles. There is a list of the officers, NCOs and men of the Yeomanry, and a detailed map entitled: 'A typical map, issued by the XIth Division

RIGHT *During the month of May, at the very bottom of the Jungle, the yellow candelabra primulas clash with the light purple of the foxgloves in a breathtaking display. The foliage of the tree ferns is also at its most beguiling at this time.*

(left flank) at Suvla Bay.' The roads, trenches and gulleys go by names such as Fleet Street, Bond Street, Hyde Park Corner, Oxford Circus, Holborn and Park Lane. There is also a signalling diagram of lines from Lone Tree Gulley at Suvla Bay, where some of the fiercest fighting took place. It is completely unintelligible to the untrained eye, and must have come back with my grandfather when he returned in December 1915. This brief photographic record of one of the most hideous campaigns in any war concludes with a telegram which reads quite simply: 'To Lady Jeane Petherick, Longford, Bodenham, Wilts. Expect arrive Southampton December 9th hospital ship *Reginadeitalia*, Gerald Petherick.' An addendum at the bottom of the telegram in my grandmother's hand reads: 'Rec'd Dec 3rd 1915.'

By January 1916 the scene in the album has switched to Heligan, now with pictures of my grandmother smiling as she looks up from her desk in the library, two huge vases of daffodils at her elbow and my Aunt Julian, as a baby, in my grandfather's arms. More pertinently there are five pages of superbly clear photographs of various different parts of the garden, including well-wooded areas below the house, showing ponds and tree ferns. This area is what has been known throughout the restoration as the Jungle.

A view from the library window on a snowy day in the week of 27 February 1916 shows the outline and dark foliage of several large conifers. A shot of the top pond from above gives further evidence of very tall conifers and already well-grown specimens of *Rhododendron arboreum* all around the pond – the same ones that kiss the surface of the water and drop their blossom on it today. A pair of mute swans glides lazily over the water. There are pictures of my grandfather and grandmother playing with Spot the dog against tree ferns that are truly mammoth – not so much in height, but in girth; they seem to be inordinately thick around the stem. Whether they are self-seeded plants or original introductions is hard to say, but they are almost certainly *Dicksonia antarctica*, the Australian and Tasmanian tree fern. W. J. Bean wrote about it, in the first edition of his definitive work, *Trees and Shrubs Hardy in the British Isles*, published in 1914, in the following terms: 'It is the only tree fern of any consequence grown out-of-doors with success in the British Isles.' He goes on to say that according to Hooker the trunks are occasionally 30–50 feet high in a wild state and as much as 50 feet in diameter. Bean adds that there are some very fine examples in the shady valley leading down to the seashore at Bosahan (one of Cornwall's best valley gardens) and that a 'notable group luxuriates in a disused quarry at Caerhays where the fern is naturalising itself freely.' There is no doubt that this extraordinary plant gives the Jungle its prehistoric feeling. The thickly wooded, steep-sided valley is dotted throughout with these strange ferns, with heads of exploding foliage and trunks that lean out from every angle, from behind which it seems possible that a dinosaur might appear at any moment.

With the Brazilian native, *Gunnera manicata*, which looks like a giant rhubarb, and the skunk cabbage, *Lysichiton americanus*, which is a native of America, the area below the third pond in the Jungle is as futuristic a garden as you are likely to see anywhere. It is a truly extraordinary sight. The bright yellow flowers of the skunk cabbage, combined with the gunnera flowers that look like small conifers in their own right, are all overseen by the intensely green new

fronds of the tree ferns in spring. In November 1915, a particularly violent gale tore through the Jungle from the south-west and laid waste large tracts of land. It is clear from the pictures taken by my grandmother that a great many trees were lost, but it is also clear that substantial replanting was carried out by February of the following year. Stump upon stump is shown sawn through with a two-man saw and many young trees are visible as replacement plantings. That gale arrived at a very inopportune moment because Jack Tremayne had answered the call of king and country and felled many of his great oaks for the war effort. It was a loyal and sacrificial move – and one he no doubt regretted – but just as the house was made available for the wounded, so the trees had to play their part.

The term 'valley garden' is one closely associated with Cornwall. Many of the larger estates have valleys leading down to the sea in which gardens have been planted over the years. The microclimate created by their aspect, the tree cover, and the downward slope which allows frost to drain through, is very suitable for growing exotic and semi-hardy plants that would otherwise survive only in the very far west of the county or the Isles of Scilly. Bosahan, Trebah and Glendurgan, which are nearly side by side on the beautiful Helford River, are outstanding in their arrays of different species, and for their awesome views through the foliage to the river. Penjerrick, close to Falmouth, is a popular favourite and takes the breath away for its hidden valley and the amazing ponds within it. At Antony, near Saltash, you cross a bridge through the valley, and reach out and smell the flowers of the huge magnolias planted 20 feet below. All beautiful and magical in their own ways, these gardens were recognised in the nineteenth century by their owners, such as the Fox family at Penjerrick, as having terrific potential for the unusual plants that were flooding in from abroad, and the valleys were landscaped and planted accordingly. The valley at Heligan is narrow, but this does not detract from the wonderful atmosphere, created by clever positioning of trees, ponds and, since the restoration, the boardwalk which circumnavigates the valley. Because it is raised, the boardwalk gives that little bit of extra height that puts you 'up there', giving the feeling that you are off the ground and in some way more connected with the great plants that surround you.

It is plain that the architects of the Jungle, but particularly Jack Tremayne, who was squire from 1901–49, had a passion for conifers – and certainly by the beginning of the twentieth century there was a wide range of conifers available for sale in various nurseries throughout England. In the foreground of one picture is what looks very much like a Monterey pine which has just been planted. Others survived that big blow to this day, and there are now magnificent specimens of *Cryptomeria japonica*, the Japanese cedar, which has the most pungent of foliage when crushed between the fingers. There are also two big monkey-puzzle trees (*Araucaria araucana*), the Chile pine, first introduced by Archibald Menzies in 1795 and then by the Cornish plant hunter William Lobb in 1844. Sadly last autumn saw the end of an enormous coastal redwood (*Sequoia sempervirens*). There is also a *Podocarpus totara*, a conifer native to the north and south islands of New Zealand, which dominates the middle section of the Jungle where the boardwalk crosses between the second and third ponds. This was an inspired planting; the tree has become truly regal in its old age, and gives the impression of holding court, right there

PREVIOUS PAGE *Looking over the top pond and down the valley garden of the Jungle, from beneath Heligan House, through the massed ranks of Rhododendron arboreum. It could only be Cornwall, and there are few views to match this.* LEFT *The ponds had all silted up and the water flowed at barely a trickle when the restoration started in 1991. Vegetative growth is still luxurious where there is ample water, rich, silty soil and little frost.* RIGHT *A photograph of my grandmother being mauled by Spot the dog, beneath two of the biggest tree ferns* (Dicksonia antarctica) *I have ever seen. The scene is the Jungle and the date 1915.*

in the centre of proceedings. There are also two maidenhair trees (*Gingko biloba*) in the Jungle, an indication that this type of tall conical tree was very much the fashion for creating structure and shape in the garden. Gingkoes are deciduous but they have a very fine skeletal shape in the winter when leafless. Fossils of their leaves found in China predate man by some 160 million years, making this the oldest species of tree by what you might call a clear margin.

The other type of plant that was planted extensively in the Jungle and which lends the place a consummate aura of the exotic is bamboo. Here we see bamboo and rhododendron grow side by side, as they are found in Nepal in the middle hills of the Himalayas. When John Nelson first laid the boardwalk that still forms the route around the Jungle, he hacked through a thick forest of *Chimonobambusa quadrangularis* and created a tunnel in the process. In the early 1990s, when funds were low, we used to make forays into the Jungle every spring to cut 400 stems of *C. quadrangularis* to use as bean poles in the Vegetable Garden. The bamboo harvest in Malaysia had failed for several years in succession and bamboo canes were at a premium and extremely expensive. It was a dreadful job that took a heavy toll on the wrists and cut you to shreds at the same time, the buds in the leaf axils being sharp as razors. But we stopped the practice when the new growth couldn't keep up with our harvesting, and rather than risk the deep density of the tunnel we resorted to imports from south-east Asia via the local garden centre.

The photographs in my grandmother's album are happy ones. According to Damaris Tremayne, niece of Jack Tremayne and aunt of the current owner of Heligan, John Willis, it appears that as close neighbours and friends my family had been given a fairly free run of the house, and probably a private wing of their own. There are pictures of snipe shooting parties and gentle rambles through the gardens. There is even one of Betty the monkey sitting on a log,

PREVIOUS PAGE *The light comes from unusual angles at the bottom of the Jungle. Sheltered and protected, it is like a lost world, often without a breath of wind as the air simply passes over the top of the tree canopy.* ABOVE LEFT *Like them or not, hydrangeas are very much 'of the country'. Here they provide ground cover below the straight, tall trunks of the chusan palm and the less linear* Rhododendron arboreum. ABOVE RIGHT *How some of the great tree ferns have survived and grown over the years is extraordinary.*

being hand-fed peanuts by an old fellow in a cap and an ankle-length apron. In another, my grandfather looks relaxed as he leans on his stick in front of the 'original *Rhododendron aucklandii*', his faithful black Labrador Spot by his side. It is impossible to imagine how hard it must have been to recover from such horrors as were seen in the Great War, but I feel sure that the generosity of the Tremaynes and the peace and magic of the gardens at Heligan contributed significantly to his recovery.

When the restoration began the Jungle was as impenetrable as its very name suggests. Self-seeded trees abounded, predominantly ash and sycamore, just as in the Northern Gardens. The ponds were silted up, and due to the steepness of the incline clearance became very difficult, particularly in the winter months. The removal of the 'weed' trees was a lengthy process as virtually every branch had to be lowered by rope in order to preserve the various shrubs and other flora that lay beneath. If four-wheel drive vehicles could not penetrate into the Jungle, at least chainsaws could. Imagine how it must have been for those without either in the nineteenth century and before. Ponds were dug by hand. Stone for the building of dams was moved by those very same hands. The working lives of the men who created the Jungle garden were hard, just as they were in the Vegetable Garden or anywhere else on the estate. I recall heartbreaking days spent in the Jungle in the depths of winter when it was too wet to

till the soil in the Vegetable Garden and we were called up to assist with the clearing. Bonfires hissed and sulked in the rain, moss-covered branches of rotting wood simply refused to burn, whilst we laboured inside oilskins, sweating and wishing we had brought some proper food down with us. Instead we had to face the haul back up the hill for 'crib', the very same word for tea break as was used by the workers who originally planted the Jungle and dug the ponds. They, however, would have been packed off to work each day by mothers and wives with a mouthwatering pasty in their crib box; most of us were not so lucky. And yet we all felt a huge sense of privilege to be working in this extraordinary landscape, to be a part of its regeneration. We trod with care, only too aware of the sleeping magic that we were reawakening. Trampling on what had lain untouched for so long, it was as though we were committing trespass; but this was a man-made landscape, and as such it needed the hand of man to bring it to life again.

The Jungle had the same magic that the walled gardens had. Not quite on the scale of Ross Island in the Andaman Islands in the Bay of Bengal – where vines and creepers had swallowed up an entire British Colonial settlement – but close enough. The copious debris was gradually removed to make way for new plantings and leave breathing space for the old. Today the Jungle garden is a new and vital place, where water flows effortlessly through unsilted ponds and down through the valley via the Old Mill, through the water meadows and finally out to

ABOVE LEFT *From the sublime to the ridiculous. The subtropical scene of the Jungle is bounded by the remainder of a crop of maize, a juxtaposition reflecting the extraordinary diversity of the gardens at Heligan.* ABOVE RIGHT *There is something about the layering of the clumps of* Rhododendron arboreum *that lends to the Jungle something of an air of the middle hills of the Himalayas; this is what you see if you go there.*

sea at Mevagissey. A copse of banana plants and swathes of canna lilies grow amongst the old rhododendrons, the great oaks, and groves of *Crinodendron*, tree ferns and bamboo. Sometimes in the evenings the silence is complete, as though the Jungle feels content with its place in the landscape.

## The Western Shelterbelt

Although it lies at a low altitude and slopes ever downward in a southerly direction towards the sea, the Jungle has every right to feel sheltered. It receives cover not only from the big trees in the grounds of Heligan House itself, but also from the western shelterbelt on the west flank of the garden. A walk through the shelterbelt is one of the return routes to the garden, and for me it is one of the most interesting and revealing. In this narrow strip of woodland you feel the extremities of Heligan. In a westerly gale it becomes unthinkable that anything could grow in the garden in the face of such punishment. It is a curious place; eerie, almost. Perhaps because it was designed to do a specific job, which was and still is to keep the wind at bay, it has

an atmosphere unlike any other part of the garden. The trees must feel the weight of such responsibility. The ash, sycamores, oaks and hollies are low-growing yet solid; they are gnarled, yet sturdy; and many of them are very old, though they remain thin and spindly. They are shelter trees and as such they are formed this way. It is a fitting tribute to the shelterbelt that the creators of the sleeping mud maid chose to site her here. This extraordinarily beautiful piece of sculpture is of a woman lying on her side with her back to the trees and the westerly wind; her hair is of montbretia and her body has been colonised by grasses, lichens and mosses; her eyes are shut, and she sleeps peacefully as the wind roars over her head and away over the top of the garden.

ABOVE *The garden abounds with types of unnamed* Rhododendron arboreum, *each one slightly different from the other whether it be in size, shape or colour, just like the many examples of* Camellia japonica *at Heligan which were also never named.*

## The Lost Valley

Of all the different areas that make up Heligan, the Lost Valley in particular emanates a sense of peace. As the land drops down to the valley floor and the landscape widens out, it is almost as if the walker is led into a dreamscape. It is otherworldly, resonating with a deep tranquillity;

PREVIOUS PAGE *Here the evening sun sinking in the west warms the back of the sleeping mud maid. Tucked away halfway up the Woodland Walk, which doubles as the western shelterbelt, she is admired by many who pass by this way.* RIGHT *The calm and tranquillity of the Lost Valley is accentuated by the width of the Georgian Ride, which runs alongside the ponds. Perhaps horses and riders would stop here in times gone by to assuage their thirst after a long morning's tour of the estate and its gardens.* BELOW *Prolific self-seeders, these foxgloves thrive in the damp and slightly acidic conditions of the woodland floor, creating a natural and spontaneous beauty.*

a very fitting end to a visit to Heligan, a resting place from which to gather the resources needed to strike out uphill for home. The vast, flat expanse of the lakes contributes greatly to this feeling of width and space, while the big oaks that surround them give a sense of enclosure, of being held, of safety. The Jungle does not have this, nor, indeed, was it supposed to. There the emphasis is on the notable non-indigenous species of tree, which were there to be displayed and admired, or on the descending ponds and their connecting bridges and pathways, which must have attracted admiration for the feats of engineering and building required to put them together. Neither do the paths down to the Lost Valley have the same comfortable feeling as the valley itself. For me the Sunken Lane, a typically high Cornish hedge of stone and scrub trees (down which I can see, in my mind's eye, the Vicar of Altarnun riding to Jamaica Inn), is a somewhat spooky path, with a sense of an approach into the unknown about it. By the time it joins Bottle Dump Hill the air has thickened and I move on as fast as I can. Just past the dump itself I can see the valley floor a hundred yards ahead and the uneasy feeling passes. It seems that the sides of the Lost Valley hold some strange energy. Even John Nelson, the hardiest of souls, felt compelled to leave the valley as fast as his legs could carry him one night some years ago. He had been working alone somewhere between the bottle dump and the east end of the valley, when his old dog Flea became unsettled, raising her hackles. John found himself in the midst of what has been loosely described as a 'black presence', and both he and the dog felt a very strong urge to get away as fast as possible. But that air of discomfort has never touched me by the lakes, nor on through the valley to the east, where the charcoal burners have been for the last year or so.

The Georgian Ride was created by Henry Hawkins Tremayne towards the end of the eighteenth century to provide easy access around his estate. It runs alongside the restored lakes and their dams and leats, which hold the water that to this day runs past the Heligan Mill farther down the valley. It is the most tranquil place imaginable. You can feel the age of the trees, the habitats and the rides, of the paths, the resting places and indeed the whole system that makes up the Lost Valley. At the bottom of the Jungle, where it meets with the Georgian Ride, there are two stone water troughs nestling side by side underneath an old stone wall. You can imagine the horses drinking deeply from the troughs after a hot morning's exercise, the water sweet from filtration by the Jungle ponds. The Lost Valley has been used for so much over such a long period of time; now that it has become a place of leisure again, it feels at peace with itself. But still it needs careful management to avoid a return to the decay that set in after the First World War.

The restoration of the Lost Valley presented an even greater task than the Jungle, so severe was the level of neglect. Through the winter of 1995/6, rather as we had done in the Jungle in previous winters, it was all hands to the pump to clear out the tangled mess in the valley floor. It seemed that there was some kind of system of lakes and leats, used to control the movement of water to Heligan Mill where corn had been ground into flour for the estate. To discover the true nature of the place meant excavation and yet more removal of weed trees such as ash and sycamore – the presence of which, and lack of oaks and other ornamental trees, indicating that

there were no trees there at all before the volunteer weeds. In fact there are few ornamental trees in the Lost Valley except for two London plane trees (*Platanus hybrida*) and a number of conifers such as the larch (*Larix decidua*).

It was a return to previous winters, when we had heaved timber around in the mud – except by this time the charcoal kilns had arrived, so the gloom of the valley floor was now further enhanced by their blue smoke. It is nearer scorching than burning, like a slow form of torture, something akin to what we were being subjected to as we paddled around in the swamp that was the valley floor. Where was the Head Gardener's Office now, and why wasn't I reading seed

PREVIOUS PAGE *The shape of these two beech trees (Fagus sylvatica) has been determined by the prevailing westerly wind, blowing from right to left on the western flank of the Lost Valley.* LEFT *Bluebells and the young foliage of ferns cover the floor of the Lost Valley in early spring. The woodland here is subject to regular thinning and replanting to avoid a return to the decay which set in after the First World War. It provides natural habitat for a number of wildlife species.*

ABOVE *Rosebay willowherb spreads its roots silently underground as well as self-seeding successfully. In late summer the air is thick with the plants' feathery seed-heads blowing in the wind.* RIGHT *Early morning light seen through a London plane tree. The foliage of this tree is an unusual sight in Cornwall. It was one of the few ornamental trees left at the start of restoration.*

catalogues in front of the fire in there? It was John Nelson who directed affairs and pushed on in determined fashion, to ascertain how this woodland fitted in to the great scheme of things. Perhaps we will never really know any more about it than we currently do.

The forest, and in our case I mean our own broad-leaved native woodland, is one of the safest self-regulating systems on the planet. A true forest has seven layers: a root zone, ground cover, shrub, small tree, large tree, canopy layer and climber. This versatility serves carnivore, herbivore, bird, mammal, insect, and all the lichen, fungi and invertebrates alike. In Asia – India, Nepal, Bangladesh, Sri Lanka – and in parts of Africa, there has long been a tradition of forest gardening. My own experience of it was fostered by several visits to the late Robert Hart's forest garden at Wenlock Edge in Shropshire, but I also worked with it in South India, where it seems to be a complete system even when tailored by man. In Tamil Nadu and Kerala there are small forest gardens around homesteads, comprising a root zone held by an edible tuber such as taro or ginger, a ground cover of perhaps a creeping squash, a few coffee bushes (because coffee in that part of the world needs shade), a small tree like pomegranate or citrus (also tolerant of shade), a large tree such as an avocado or a silk cotton tree and a canopy tree such as a rosewood. The climber would be pepper or betel nut, the areca vine. Under this management the monsoon rains are withstood, run-off is minimal, and there is food for all. The system may be better suited to the humid tropics than southern England, but it nonetheless works in temperate climates such as the Lost Valley, where the plants and the ecosystem are robust and healthy.

This system provides habitation for a number of bird species. Perhaps the rumours of sightings of a little egret are true. It is only a matter of time before this companionable little member of the heron family takes up residence at Heligan as the Lost Valley offers its ideal habitat: abundant water with trees by its edge for nesting. Sheet-white with distinct

PREVIOUS PAGE *Looking
north-east along the Lost
Valley over the old stew
ponds. The absence of
mature trees suggests that
the pond in the distance
once fed into the now
overgrown foreground.*
RIGHT *The proliferation
of ferns throughout the
woodlands of the south-west
of England is one of the
great joys of our temperate
climate.* OPPOSITE PAGE
Pulsatilla vulgaris, *the
pasque-flower. This flower
is beautiful but shy, and
growing at ground level,
it requires dropping to
the knees for a closer
look in order to really
appreciate its charms.*

yellow legs, the egret has a very spectre-like appearance, seeming to float through the air in a manner akin to a lapwing. It is particularly active in the early evening on the upper reaches of the Fowey River past Golant and up towards Lerryn. There are resident pairs there and, increasingly, all over the south of England; some have bred, and it looks as though this native of Asia and Africa has found a new home in the British Isles. The kingfisher, another prominent waterside bird, is also an honorary native – it should really be called the Eurasian kingfisher. It is never likely to be present in numbers as there is simply not enough room, but to hear the shrill pipe of the blue flash as it whizzes by on its way to another perch is a veritable ornithological treat. It is the impermanence of it, the tease, wherein lies the pleasure.

The woodland throughout the Lost Valley is subject to regular thinning and replanting of broad-leaved trees. As we are no longer able to rely on our stock of bamboo to supply the gardens, we have returned to the age-old practice of coppicing hazel for the production of bean poles and pea sticks. The word coppice comes from the Norman-French *couper*, meaning to cut. If a broad-leaved tree is cut back to a stump or 'stool' it will send up shoots from side buds just above the ground. It is then called a coppiced tree because it does not have one single trunk. In the case of hazel each stool is harvested every seven to ten years, before the poles get too big to drive into the ground; this process can continue for up to a hundred years. It is a very fitting arena in which to catch a breath before making the long haul back up to the gardens, and it is well worth lingering for the blue flash of a kingfisher over the lakes, or to hear the sweet song of a blackcap. But in the high summer, when the nesting season is over and the scrapping for territory is forgotten, the silence can be total, just as in the Jungle.

The Wider Heligan

# 2 Fauna

*Animal life would not exist on earth without oxygen – it is hard to get a better reason for growing a tree than that. Yet trees give us so much more: shelter, fuel, medicine, food, fertiliser, clean water; the list is endless.*

# The Wider
# Heligan

LEFT *South Devon bullocks and Poll Dorset ewes graze quietly in Higher Beef Park which lies below the Northern Summerhouse, with St Austell Bay away in the distance to the east.* ABOVE *Allium hollandicum 'Purple Sensation', which has been planted to encourage insect life around the pond in front of the bird hide. Other species planted in order to stimulate wildlife include* Rosa rugosa *and* Mahonia aquifolium.

The wider estate begins with a peek over the *Griselinia* hedge at the Northern Summerhouse. The landscape opens up and falls gently away to the sea no more than a mile and half away as the crow flies. But it is not the nearby beach at Pentewan that is in the frame – it is the open expanse of St Austell Bay and the Gribbin Head that gives such a feeling of space. In the foreground the folds of the land intertwine to reveal the part of Heligan that lies outside the garden walls, and is waiting to be explored.

## The Wood Project

Whilst the produce from the walled gardens finds its way to the tea room, finished and unfinished products from our trees also find homes both on and off the estate. Andy Giles and Irving Sweet are the men to be seen operating the mobile saw bench, which is housed on the eastern flank of the gardens where machinery is kept and the staff have their crib room. Our 'Whole Tree Policy' is the practice of ensuring that every possible part of a tree felled on the estate is used to maximum effect. All waste is pollution; if this maxim is at the forefront of thinking, it is much easier to use an abundant natural resource such as a tree in the correct manner. A huge amount of timber is processed and used for many things, from bole blanks for turning, to planks for garden furniture.

Throughout the ages trees have been used in a multitude of ways. Even at the most basic level green leaves, by their very act of growing, produce the oxygen we breathe. This photosynthesis is quite simply the way in which a green leaf takes carbon dioxide from the atmosphere, then combines it with water and light and turns it into oxygen. Animal life would not exist on earth without oxygen – it is hard to get a better reason for growing a tree than that. Yet trees give us so much more: shelter, food, medicine, fuel, fertiliser, soil stability, clean water, animal habitats; the list is endless. Their place in the landscape alone is a source of great joy. There are trees at Heligan which are well over two hundred years old; how majestic they look and how venerable they seem, creating an atmosphere around them of wisdom, knowledge and understanding. It is therefore right and proper that all trees – from the great oaks down to the sapling sycamore that has to be weeded out – are given maximum respect and put to full use, for without trees we are nothing.

One species of tree which is a common sight in the woodlands of the south-west of England is the holly (*Ilex aquifolium*). When the project at Heligan first started and clearance of the garden was moving ahead, a large number of holly trees were removed and sawn up. At that time wood-turning hobbyists began to appear, showing a strong interest in the wood from holly, and also rhododendron, for fashioning various different artefacts. To this day one of my most prized possessions is a 'dibber' (a small, pointed hand tool for pricking out seedlings), beautifully crafted from a piece of holly by one of the early wood-turners. I have had it for ten years, and carry it with me whenever I am gardening.

The evergreen holly is a particularly hard wood. It burns hot and slow even when 'green', and the tree produces beautiful red berries which we use for decoration. It has long been used as living stock-proof fencing and, with ivy, is the subject of a famous Christmas carol, to name

BELOW *Purple loosestrife* (Lythrum salicaria)*, one of our prettiest wild flowers which has now begun to make a name for itself as a garden-worthy plant.* OPPOSITE *Morning light through the Lost Wood, which is the home of nest boxes for barn owls and countless other species of bird which nest in and around this forest. The contents of these boxes can be seen on screens in Horsemoor Hide, courtesy of eco-watch.*

but one song. On Twelfth Night, when the Christmas decorations come down, it crackles splendidly on the bonfire, the ash from which can be used on the garden as a form of potash. Holly trees are still in evidence in the woods throughout the estate. They are easily propagated by birds – blackbirds and thrushes in particular – who strip the tree of berries and deposit them elsewhere, resulting in new trees. And that is just the holly, not one of the long-living giants of the English landscape, but one which is etched into our minds as a classic – with a very ancient history, reaching as far back, some say, as the crown of thorns worn by Christ at his crucifixion.

There are around one thousand, five hundred species of tree which can be found in England today, and we can thank a handful of people, the Tremaynes among them, for the arrival of

many of these from the days of the plant hunters and before. Our native trees are few in number because of our island's separation from the continent after the last Ice Age some eight thousand years ago, but they do include some of the greats, such as oak, ash, beech and yew. The woodlands around the Heligan estate are predominantly made up of the first three, with sizeable populations of willow, hazel, holly and blackthorn. The imported sycamore, which came from France in the Middle Ages and so may have been an English native before the Ice Age, is also prominent. These trees are primarily the ones that we have to decide how best to

utilise. Thinning, replanting, chipping, pruning for safety reasons, coppicing hazel for garden peasticks, burning, turning or making into furniture are all activities that can be seen in the management of the woodlands at Heligan. Leaving stacks of logs throughout the Lost Valley to create wildlife habitats is also an important part of the health of a wood and the fauna that it supports. The forest floor is one of the few places where soil builds itself up; indeed the forest is a very stable and balanced environment.

To give an indication of the diverse uses of some native species of tree at Heligan we can look at our Pineapple Pit in the Melon Yard. For centuries oak trees have been used for the extraction of tannin to tan the hides of animals. When a pile of oak bark chippings used for tanning is left for a certain amount of time, a fermenting process takes place, and it is this which provided the heat around the pineapple pots as they overwintered in their pit. Once the heat had subsided the bark could be used as a mulch, as a surface for a path, or could be left to rot down further before being added to the soil in the form of compost. Sadly, the tannery in the nearby village of Grampound no longer supplies us with tan bark, so we now plunge our pineapple pots in freshly chipped material from prunings around the estate.

## The Orchards

Whilst the ornamental trees in the garden were considered special by the Victorians, and the trees of the shelterbelts and woodlands vital, the importance of fruit-bearing trees to an estate the size of Heligan cannot be underestimated. Not only did the trees bear precious fruit, they also offered shelter for animals – notably ewes, which in a hard winter may have lambed in the orchard due to its shelter and proximity to the farmhouse. The rams may also have spent some time there, particularly in the summertime when they could feed on the rich grass and shelter in the shade of the trees before the tupping season. The farm's beehives may have been sited in the orchard, again providing shelter for the bees and giving them direct access to blossom, allowing them to stimulate the pollination of the fruit crops.

The primary crop of the orchard was the apple – for dessert, cooking, cider and even for pickling purposes (pickled apples were served at Sunday tea as a treat). But apple cultivation in Cornwall has never been straightforward. It is interesting that only one orchard has ever been made mention of at Heligan, on a tithe map dating as far back as 1770, situated between the house and the Jungle. Today we have planted two orchards, one behind Shepherd's Barn next to the Wood Project, and another which runs behind the Old Wood, below the Old Kennels. Both are devoted primarily to varieties of Cornish apple, but to these have been added a

PREVIOUS PAGE *The bee hives are tucked away from the wind and sheltered by the big oak trees, as the land begins to fall away towards Bottle Dump Hill and the Lost Valley.* LEFT *The orchard, made up of Cornish apple varieties, is sheltered by the Lost Wood, which here casts its morning shadow. The buildings of Peruppa Farm are visible at the top right of the picture.*

number of cherry trees, whose ancestors once formed part of a booming cherry industry in the Tamar Valley (which divides Cornwall from its neighbouring county, Devon).

A great number of apples would have been grown and eaten in Cornwall by our forebears, despite the difficulties associated with the growing of top fruit in the county due to its climatic conditions. Apples like their summers sunny and dry. This is why they are grown in Kent and pockets of Worcestershire and Berkshire, which are in rain shadows and are therefore 'hot spots'. The warm, damp climate of Cornwall creates ideal conditions for the spread of major diseases which affect apples: canker, scab and mildew. Pests such as aphid and codling moth also thrive in the warm climate, where they are able to overwinter rather than having their populations reduced as they would in the cooler climes. Add to this the acidity of Cornish soils, not forgetting the need for trees to withstand the ravages of the winds that can plague the peninsula through the winter months, and it is apparent that it was because of these problems that so many indigenous varieties of Cornish apple evolved over the centuries.

It must be pointed out here that the apples which grow down the central path of the Vegetable Garden and on the walls of the Melon Yard are not Cornish varieties, but were carefully selected for their ability to endure West Country conditions. The exception is the very first apple at the top of the Vegetable Garden, Devonshire Quarrenden, from which a whole series of Cornish apples are descended.

Until the Second World War most farms in Cornwall boasted an area of two or three acres given over to orchard, enough to suggest that tree fruit was an important component of the home economy. Just as with vegetables, trialling of varieties became essential. The practice was to sow apple seeds in the garden, and then plant the tree out in the hedgerows. The ability of an apple tree to withstand wind rock was, and still is, very important. Even today, if a tree is not securely staked, exposure to wind creates rocking, from which follows a smoothing of the sides of the hole in which it is planted. This in turn allows rainwater into the hole and drowns the tree; this is known in the trade simply as 'the Death'. As the tree matured the fruiting potential could be assessed and, if satisfactory, the tree was lifted and brought to the orchard.

Traditionally, and as is the case at Heligan today, the orchard apples were grown on 'free' (seedling) rootstocks, which give maximum vigour and allow the tree to grow to its chosen size. The trees also remain unpruned in order to reduce the chances of infection from canker. These are the gnarled old apple trees of romantic fiction, that bend in age and fatten the lambs or pigs that graze below them. And with them come a collection of names to match: Blackamoor Red, Manaccan Primrose and Lord of the Isles.

Standing in an authentic Cornish orchard takes me back to childhood, to a time when particular apples would be greatly anticipated before being made into specific dishes, or simply eaten straight from the tree. When I was young my father made Cornish cream; this was one of the only possible reasons to come up from the beach on time: to eat dinner and then relish the stewed apple and cream that followed.

My own personal favourite is Cornish Gilliflower, an apple that is quite widespread in its cultivation in England and probably one of the best around. It does not ripen until late October

but is well worth the wait; it is very crispy to bite into, with a flavour as rich and aromatic as any apple you have ever tasted. There is a Gilliflower growing in amongst the camellias in my parents' garden at Porthpean, with only two James Grieve and a very spicy apple called Sops in Wine for company. I say Sops in Wine, but stand to be corrected – a number of apples have been given this name throughout history. Also at Porthpean are two trees of a variety we know simply as the Christmas apple, because it stores until then. It is, in fact, called John Standish, and whilst not Cornish in the least, having been raised at Ascot in Berkshire in 1871, it is an apple that does particularly well in Cornwall where many others fail.

Among the trees in the orchards at Heligan, as well as Gilliflower, is Ben's Red. A small, striking red apple, it is unusual because it is one of a number of Cornish varieties that produces roots on its stem at the junctions of branches. Known as pitchers, these negated the need for grafting the variety on to selected rootstocks. It was, and very often still is, how Ben's Red and its excellent relation Red Roller propagated. The branch holding the small, dormant adventitious roots is removed from the tree and planted. It is a similar practice to pinning down strawberry runners at leaf junctions, where they too produce roots.

The resurgence of the Cornish apple has been the work of a small band of enthusiasts. None have worked harder than Mary Martin and James Armstrong Evans, who live at St Dominick in the Tamar Valley. They have reintroduced countless varieties and prevented many others from disappearing from cultivation altogether. All those with an interest in Cornish apples owe them a great debt of thanks. Their story is told by Mary's sister Virginia Spiers in a book beautifully illustrated by Mary called *Burcombes, Queenies and Colloggetts*, published by West Brendon.

What they have done for the Cornish apple also goes for the Cornish cherry, and we have a number of cherry trees in the Poultry Orchard at Heligan that bear witness to this, namely Birchenhayes, Bullion, Burcombe and Fice. In a manner somewhat similar to the apple, the cherries of the Tamar Valley had to adapt to the thin soils of the steep-sided river valleys and the wetter climate, a problem that often results in splitting of the fruit. However, the warmer temperatures of the south-west allowed the crop to ripen early, which meant it had an advantage over its rivals in the far south-east of England. By the time rail transport had become efficient the fruit was sent to Plymouth by boat, and from there to London, where it was traded at Covent Garden market.

Today cherries are grown on less vigorous rootstocks that suit the picking of the fruit and the management of the trees. In the early part of the twentieth century, when the cherry industry was booming in the Tamar Valley, the fruit was picked by men who scampered through the enormous trees like squirrels, having reached the uppermost branches by way of a huge thirty- or forty-rung ladder. There is one such ladder hanging under the eaves of the lean-to in the Melon Yard, but that was probably used for tree surgery and reaching the tops of walls rather than picking cherries. Nevertheless it certainly has enough rungs and the weight of it is astonishing. Such was the sight of the cherry blossom in the spring that paddle steamers carried day trippers from Plymouth to see it. The industry no longer survives, but there remains a strong tradition of market gardening on the fertile sides of the Tamar and its tributaries.

## Poultry

Whilst the ducks, geese and poultry that run beneath the apples and cherries in the Poultry Orchard attract attention from many passing visitors, they also fulfil an important role in the health of the orchard itself. Not only do they manure the ground and produce delicious 'free range' eggs, the grass colouring their yolks a rich orange, they also clean the ground of unwanted pests that might otherwise overwinter in windfall apples.

The Appleyard ducks, which look very similar to mallards, are renowned as slug eaters, as are their close relations the Khaki Campbells. The Marans, dark spotted hens, are exceptional layers which produce the large brown eggs that have only been popular in England since

between the wars, while perhaps the stars of the show are the large beige hens called Buff Orpingtons. It is hard to believe that this great big bumbling bird is descended from the junglefowl that still roams wild in parts of India. I was fortunate enough to catch the occasional glimpse of it when I worked on the subcontinent. The cock is a brightly coloured bird, which is secretive but curious about humans and would often venture around the homesteads before dawn. This bird has the loudest early-morning crow of any fowl that I have heard. Rhode Island Reds are also present in the orchard in order to boost the laying ranks, being very reliable egg producers.

## The Farm and Rare Breeds

As the project of restoring Heligan has progressed, the huge web of connections that binds the different parts of the estate together is gradually being re-established. As a self-contained estate Heligan would have been at the height of its powers by the mid to late nineteenth century. Certainly some external produce would have been brought in, but even bananas and pineapples were produced at Heligan, and it has to be said that few of us manage to attain such heights today. We have shown in our productive gardens how high quality food was and still is produced, albeit at a high cost and for the privileged

PREVIOUS PAGE *The coastline of south Cornwall remains largely unspoiled, as this view eastwards over Heligan's Home Farm and further up the coast indicates.* BELOW *Five Poll Dorset ewes and a single lamb, their woolly foreheads clearly visible, take an interest in the photographer whilst grazing Higher Beef Park. They are owned and farmed by the Lobb family to exacting standards.*

few in the Victorian era. With the management of the land outside the gardens, however, it is a different story. Farming as we know it today is highly industrialised, almost entirely mechanised and geared specifically to maximum output, often with minimal input. One hundred and fifty years ago it could not have been more different. An estate the size of Heligan would have supported a large agricultural community providing shelter, food, fuel and employment. Today the country is faced with plummeting land-based incomes and declining rural economies. The health of our land is poor and in most cases our crops are dependent upon chemical inputs for growth.

Since the beginning of chemical farming, there has been a one-way movement of minerals: from the soil into plants, animals and human beings, and then out to the seas. We no longer recycle minerals on the land, except for nitrogen, phosphate and potash, and

ABOVE *A stand that any racehorse trainer would be proud of, from one of Brian Reynolds' Dartmoor ponies: all four legs evenly spaced and visible! These ponies play an important role in the maintenance of the wetland pastures of the valley floor.*

these usually in the form of standard fertilisers that do not contain the full spectrum of necessary minerals. As a result soils in Western agriculture are becoming deficient in most minerals. If they are not present in the soil, they are not in the plants, and so however healthy a diet we choose, we ourselves will become mineral-deficient. Just as we have shown in our productive gardens that it is possible to increase soil fertility by the correct practices of crop rotation and the addition of organic matter to the soil, so it is vital to our project that crops are produced and animals reared on the farmland of Heligan with time-honoured traditions brought to the fore.

The Tremayne estate, with Heligan at its core, still has land which is tenanted out to farmers, but the only remaining farm buildings at Heligan itself are those at Peruppa, sited between Tregiskey Cross, at the top of Pentewan Hill, and the entrance to the gardens. There is no longer a farmer in residence and the farmhouse is now a private dwelling, run as a bed and breakfast. The land below Peruppa, which faces towards Heligan, is the last area of south-facing land on the estate, and it is hoped that in the future this land may be brought into cultivation for arable crops. The need for farmers to learn new skills and to diversify into other areas of production is of paramount importance if small farms are to survive. The livestock industry is in ruins and the steep-sided land of many Cornish farms such as Peruppa are unsuitable for the cultivation of grain crops, which require the use of heavy machinery, often in unsuitable weather conditions.

Halfway between Heligan and my home at Porthpean, along the coast road which runs from Pentewan to St Austell, is a small row of cottages. These have always been known as Lobb's Shop because one of the end buildings was occupied by a Mr Lobb, the blacksmith. Some six generations ago one of the blacksmith's sons decided to take up farming, renting land from the Tremayne Estate at a place known as Kestle. Adjoining Heligan to the west, Kestle has grown to over eight hundred acres and is still farmed, and now owned, by three brothers, direct descendants of the blacksmith. The sheep that graze Heligan fields are from the Lobbs' flock of Poll Dorsets, and the friendly, red-coated South Devon cattle that graze Higher Beef Park, below the Northern Summerhouse, are all owned and managed by the Lobb family. The products from these animals will very soon be available from Lobbs Farm Shop and Heligan Countryside Barn,which has been built on land owned by the Lobbs that Heligan leases for use as its overflow car park.

The planning process involved in the building of this new development was inevitably a long and tiring one for the brothers, but they recognise, and are keen to share with the consumer, the fact that for farmers to survive in the climate of globalisation, free trade and supermarket dominance they have to farm sustainably and show complete accountability for the way they work their land. This fits neatly with the desire of Heligan to show correct practice in the way it manages its own land and to bring an understanding to the visitor of how food is produced outside of the productive gardens. Indeed, planning permission for the shop was only granted on the condition that the design should be fully based on correct interpretation of the land and suitable farming practices. The siting of the shop will provide a potentially high customer base for the Lobbs, while also showing how the animals that graze the fields of Heligan are managed and eventually slaughtered and butchered for consumption.

Today most of us are as far removed from our source of food as it is possible to be. It should not take another national disaster such as the outbreak of foot and mouth disease in 2001, which brought livestock farming in England to its knees, to bring food production back into the public domain. Lobbs Farm Shop and the productive gardens at Heligan together offer a huge amount of information about how food was produced, and is produced today. Peter Stafford, Heligan's managing director, likes to think of Heligan as showing the best of the old and the best of the new. We employ the same methods of building soil fertility as a head gardener in 1860, but we also use the latest biological controls to prevent damage from pests and diseases that were not available to him. Just as balance is integral to the protection of ecosystems, so it is integral to our work at Heligan. As well as striving for harmony between old and new, we must also strike a balance between showing what we believe to be the best way to manage the land, and at the same time running a popular visitor attraction.

Although the Lobbs are responsible for the sheep and cattle which graze our pasture there are still some animals that are reared by Heligan, headed by two very fine Oxford Sandy Black sows. These are a three-way cross between black Berkshire, Tamworth and Gloucester Old Spot pigs, and despite being hybrids they are in fact a breed in their own right. They are shunted around the outer estate as they are excellent for clearing ground in mature woodland. They grub out brambles and eat the roots, leaving the tops to die, thus providing invaluable assistance to the estate team. This year the two sows farrowed a total of fifteen piglets, nine gilts (females) and six boars. They are weaned at eight weeks and kept apart from twenty weeks to prevent any crossbreeding. The boars are then fattened up for sale in the Lobbs' shop or the tea room.

Brian Reynolds, the man responsible for the pigs, also keeps a number of ponies on the estate, operating from his base in the Old Kennels, where the gun dogs were kept in the days when there was a pheasant shoot at Heligan. Brian's purebred Dartmoor and Bodmin Moor ponies help with grassland management and are ideal animals for grazing the wetland pastures on the valley floor beyond Heligan Mill. The cloven-footed pig or cow would render the ground a mudbath, whereas the ponies tread lightly. Also, the ponies tend to concentrate their grazing on grass, whereas cattle will pick out plants, often important wildflowers, to supplement their diet. Even the humble moorland pony has its place in the conservation plan and its own contribution to make towards diversity at Heligan.

## The Wildlife Project

Bringing wildlife to the visitor and taking the visitor to the wildlife has become one of the most important parts of Heligan for those who venture beyond the garden gates and into the outer estate. Horsemoor Hide is now an essential stopping point on the way to the Jungle or the Lost Valley. This is a fully functioning bird hide, complete with viewing slits and one-way

glass, through which the visitor can watch bird and insect activity on the pond and at feeders. As anyone with a passing interest in ornithology will know, it is hard to get close to the birds and mammals which inhabit farmland and woodland unless there is quiet, stillness and even camouflage. Some species of bird, such as robins, blackbirds and song thrushes, are relatively tame, but there is little chance of getting close to a mixed flock of seed-eating finches (made up of siskins, twites, linnets and redpolls).

This understanding has led to an area of eight acres of semi-improved grassland being given over to the Wildlife Project. Known as Horsemoor Meadow, the area is situated to the south-east of the hide and adjacent to the Lost Wood, which runs from the bird hide to the Lost Valley. The idea is to experiment with different ways of managing grassland to encourage wildlife. For example, on one area some topping will take place annually to encourage the short-tailed field vole, which is a favourite food of the barn owl, a species which is a resident of Heligan. Most of the land is cut for hay as late as August to allow the wildflowers to set and disperse their seed. This also provides excellent habitat for butterflies, invertebrates and other fauna, as well as late-season forage for honey and bumble bees, ladybirds, spiders and burnet moths. Two acres is being reseeded with seed from an unimproved Dartmoor hay meadow, as with diversity in plant species will come wider diversity in wildlife. It has long been a contentious issue that at the hands of farmers the changing landscape deprives us of our true countryside, with natural habitats and many thousand miles of hedgerows destroyed. Hay meadows have declined to a great extent, with up to 90 per cent lost to the blades of the silage cutter in recent years. With their disappearance the skylark has suffered, as the grass is cut for silage at the end of May and beginning of June, right in the middle of the nesting season. Although silage for the feeding of housed beef cattle over winter dominates, grass is still grown for hay. In Cornwall this is rarely cut before the middle of July, thus avoiding the nesting season of most birds. The Horsemoor Meadow therefore also demonstrates what a hay meadow actually looks like, offering a wonderful historical recreation of how many of the fields at Heligan were before the advent of modern methods of farming.

Jenny King and her colleague Dave Hunter have been instrumental in setting up these projects. Both are deeply passionate about wildlife, which they seek to protect and encourage. Between them they have also set up two self-guided trails for the visitor, a Wild Plants Trail and a Mammal Discovery Trail. Both are circular walks and the accompanying leaflets indicate where the visitor might expect to come across particular plants or the droppings of certain mammals. Shapes of footprints are given for identification purposes, with approximate sizes.

While Jenny is particularly concerned with the badger sett at the top of the Lost Valley, Dave is a connoisseur of bats. In the roof of the Stewardry above Dave and Jenny's office there exists a large colony of pipistrelle bats. The smallest of the native bats, weighing only half an ounce, the colony had reached over three hundred in number by mid July 2003 as the season's young swelled the ranks. The numbers had reduced down to only forty by the middle of August, and the colony has near enough dispersed for the mating season (autumn) and winter hibernation in woods, caves and the cavity walls of buildings. Unsure whether there is any sole reason for the dispersal, Dave suggests that natural thinning as well as parasites thriving in the warm, muggy conditions of the roof space may be responsible. In addition to the pipistrelle there are also Daubenton's, noctule, horseshoe and brown long-eared bats present in numbers on the estate, along with a colony of horseshoe bats resident in Heligan House. This summer's bat evening was a great success during which, with the aid of a bat detector, Dave was able to pick up the echo-location of a bat and connect it to a frequency enabling the human ear to hear the sound they make whilst flying at night.

Some of the grassland below the Horsemoor Hide has been planted with mixed native species of tree such as birch, rowan and hazel to encourage birds to settle closer to it. The area around the hide and at the pond edge is planted with suitable species such as *Rosa rugosa* and *Mahonia aquifolium* to provide food, especially in the winter. As the woodland begins to grow it will allow more potential for cameras to show yet more coverage of the extraordinary world of the unseen. Live footage of barn owls, badgers, pipistrelle bats and any amount of nesting birds may often be seen on the fifteen television screens placed throughout the hide, via a vast network of cameras hidden in nest boxes and nooks and crannies all over the estate. There are currently over forty bird boxes dotted in and around the Lost Wood, twenty of which have hidden cameras inside. These have been set up and are monitored by Luke Sanger and Lisa Philips of eco-watch. A chance meeting at the South West Bird Fair in 1999 between Peter Stafford, Heligan's managing director, and the eco-watch team led to the first camera in the Lost Wood showing live pictures of blue tits nesting in a box. After this modest beginning Horsemoor Hide was built in 2001 and now, with underground cables running all over the outer estate, it will soon be possible to take a camera to the action and show it on a screen in the hide. A large plasma screen is following the life of a large badger sett which lies between the Sunken Lane, which leads to the Lost Valley, and Bottle Dump Hill.

Like them or not, badgers do make enthralling viewing in the flesh, and the coverage of their nocturnal activities via infrared cameras on the screen in the hide is riveting. As much as any other wild mammal, fox included, the badger incites heated debate about what we must now call the 'countryside'. Broadly speaking, farmers don't like badgers. They tear up the ground, make a terrible mess rolling around in fields of corn and eating the ripe grain, and are accused of passing bovine tuberculosis back to cattle. Gamekeepers don't like them because they are deadly to a population of young pheasants in a pen, and gardeners definitely don't want them setting up home in the garden. Yet they find a place in the nation's warm hearts as a large, bumbling mammal which should be protected. They should be safe at Heligan.

Perhaps the highlight of the Heligan wildlife project has been charting the progress of the barn owls that live on the estate. There is something hauntingly eerie about the low glide and languorous flap of the barn owl in the twilight. Its call is a terrifying screech, heard from early evening right into the depths of the night. Combined with its fondness for roosting and nesting in churches and tumbledown farm buildings, something of a ghostly aura has grown up around it. Although geographically more widespread than the tawny owl, the genuine 'tawit-tawoo' owl, barn owls are much less numerous. Modern farming practices can claim a hand in the demise of this stunning bird; many old barns are now new living spaces for humans, and the lack of rough pasture on farms has led to a decline in numbers of the small rodents on which the barn owl feeds. They are also very susceptible to danger from moving cars, as they often fly low over roads at night whilst hunting over verges. However the permanent pasture for the rearing of beef cattle and herds of milking cows that prevails in the south-west are good hunting grounds for the barn owl, and assist in arresting the decline of the species, so there is reason for hope.

There has been a barn owl roosting in one of the old barns around Heligan for some years, and it has now become possible to trace the movements of both parents and offspring via technology provided by eco-watch. In 2001 nest boxes with hidden cameras inside were put up in the Lost Wood beneath Horsemoor Hide, and for the second season in succession a pair of barn owls reared a successful brood. The boxes are designed with a baffle to prevent the chicks falling out, and are suitably sited with perches close at hand (the perch and dive form of hunting is a favourite of the barn owl). This season the male, an old bird, was radio-tagged, enabling his whereabouts to be located at all times. He has continued to use his old haunt in some nearby barns for roosting. At the beginning of the nesting season he invited a new female into a nesting box where she laid five eggs, the first on 1 May. The female then took up the role of chief incubator and sat on the eggs, while the male bird hunted and fed her continuously. She did not leave the nest from the time the eggs were laid until the chicks fledged. On 4 June the first chick hatched, to great delight. Three chicks hatched in all. After six weeks all three were ringed and after eight weeks they fledged. They will remain on the estate for a short while after fledging, then slowly they will disperse and

RIGHT *A bird whose fortunes are a constant source of fluctuating reports, the barn owls seem to enjoy the coverage they have been receiving. A successful brood raised this season is a very encouraging sign of their future at Heligan.* BELOW *The tail of a recently caught victim is just visible in the intersection of the two branches. The permanent pasture and many areas of rough*

*grass at Heligan, with its rich and diverse wildlife, provide ample feeding opportunities for the owls.* LEFT *The sturdy feet of the nuthatch allow it to range through broad-leaved trees, clinging to trunks and branches in search of small insects on which to feed.*

find new homes for themselves, possibly many miles away, wherever they can find land to hunt over and places in which to roost.

The tour guides who gather in the offices before setting off with their coach parties around the gardens have up-to-the-minute details of the progress of the barn owl family and take the joyful news to the eager visitors. It is a very strong indication of how the conservation of relatively rare forms of wildlife, such as the barn owl, is now of great consequence to people in this country, especially those who are likely to visit a place such as Heligan. However it is important that the successful rearing of young by barn owls, or any other endangered species, is seen in its wider context. The provision of habitats and the overall management of the land to produce a stable environment for all sorts of animal life, both wild and domestic, for pleasure and the kitchen, is one of the most pressing problems we face today. How it can be accomplished with economic viability presents an enormous challenge, and one that we will continue to explore. The health of the land and the people and animals that inhabit it are entirely dependent upon good practice.

It is fortunate that most of the farmland at Heligan is put down to permanent pasture, often bounded by either Cornish hedging or woodland. Both provide good habitats for birds and mammals for roosting, nesting and feeding. It is also fortunate that the Wildlife Project extends throughout the gardens at Heligan and is not restricted to the wider estate alone. It is designed to show that it is possible to run both an estate and a visitor attraction in tandem with conservation and diversity. Working with rather than against nature is the most important thing. When the garden lay asleep under its protective coat of bramble it was indeed a haven for myriad species of birds and mammals. But after the restoration the resultant widening in the diversity of plant species has also seen the return of many kinds of wildlife, particularly birds. The flocks of chaffinches and goldfinches that feed on the last few remaining seed-heads of helichrysum or globe artichokes in the Vegetable Garden are often accompanied in the autumn by bramblings. Swallows nest each year in the eaves of the Melon House. A pair of pied wagtails has for the last several seasons successfully reared broods in a cavity in the Pineapple Pit wall, despite constant attention from visitors who stand and stare in amazement. Environmental awareness is at the forefront of so much in our daily lives and the Wildlife Project, with its hidden cameras and careful explanations of land and habitat management, can only enhance people's understanding of the natural world. It may also encourage visitors to play their part in helping to sustain species diversity, even if it is just something as simple as hanging up a feed sock in the back garden.

BELOW *Badgers emerge from their sett to begin the evening's feeding. An enchanting animal to watch, especially in its antics with its young, it is* much less so if allowed *to colonise cultivated farmland and gardens. The sett is sited between Sunken Lane and Bottle Dump Hill. The nocturnal* activities of this large *and fascinating group can be viewed via infrared cameras, located all around their habitat and linked to screens in Horsemoor Hide.*

# Conclusion

As this book concludes it is late September. The maize that has stood through the long, dry summer in the fields on the side of Pentewan Hill is finally being harvested for silage to be fed to livestock through the winter. The huge machines scythe their way through a crop that was fed to cattle in the summer in Victorian times, when all was done by hand. Now this crop is attaining increasing notoriety for its association with the genetic modification of plants, about as far removed from the agriculture of one hundred and fifty years ago as is possible. How life has changed in such a short period of history in agriculture and horticulture alone.

The direct relationship between man and the land that is at the very core of the project at Heligan was integral to its ability to capture the imagination of visitors in the early days. As I see the maize cutter going about its work, it seems inconceivable that the entire crop can be cut by one man on a machine and hauled away by another. One hundred and fifty years ago it would have taken a multitude of men to do the job, the same men that might have worked in the garden at Heligan, or delivered the manure to the garden from the stables. All these connections are forgotten today; let us hope we have gone some way down the road to making them again.

The Crown Inn at St Ewe is a small, attractive Cornish inn, only a mile or so from the garden gates of Heligan. It is found directly opposite the church, in the graveyard of which is the war memorial upon which are carved many of the names of the Heligan gardeners who fell in the First World War. The landlord of The Crown is John Nelson, one of the founding fathers of the restoration of Heligan. Running a pub is another suitable role for John, although it is mainly in the kitchen he is to be found, rather than behind the bar as one might imagine. On the ground John was definitely the guv'nor. Not because he bossed everyone about (he didn't), nor because he smoked more than anyone else (which he did by a long way); it was because he worked harder than anybody else and his devotion to the garden was absolute.

If you quiz John on the reasons for the success of the project he could bring up a very long list. There is no doubt that Heligan is quite simply a beautiful and magical place, but at the top of John's list would be the sympathetic manner with which the early pioneers carried out their work. So many of the marvels of nature were left undisturbed. Yet at the same time the garden was restored to the extent that the working practices of the nineteenth century could be carried out on a daily basis by staff who could be seen doing it, be quizzed about it and often be congratulated for it. Those who cut the maize on Pentewan Hill one hundred and fifty years ago may have been the very men who planted potatoes in the fields around Heligan or cabbages in the Vegetable Garden. At times it feels as though they still are. Charles Fleming, his

shock of white hair ever visible as he scratches away at the weeds in the Vegetable Garden, is always telling visitors that he has been at Heligan since Victorian times and that he is still on Victorian wages.

As we got under way it was obvious that the project was evolving as a natural process. There was no logic to what we were doing, yet each step was logical. Our motivation proved absolutely crucial, and there was so much of it that to outsiders it must have been astonishing. It was not until years later that visitors began to say how lucky we were to work in such a beautiful garden. Certainly the motivation was not financial, and with long hours and abysmal weather in winter the rational inclination would have been to stay at home. But we kept going because above all it was terrific fun, completely original and totally lacking in rigidity, formality and bureaucracy. There were no committees, thank goodness – they are not, as a rule, tainted by inspiration – and we were significantly free from planning procedures that might well have held us back. This freedom allowed for individuals to make their presence felt and to take enormous pride in their work.

It was this determination to do things properly, the way it was done in 1850, combined with the attention paid to the authenticity of the restoration that enchanted the public in the early days; this, and the fact that the work was done at a tremendously fast rate. If it had not been so, the whole garden would have been swallowed up by the wilds once more. When nature threatened to muscle her way in again, and she often did, John would sound the rallying cry; everyone would drop everything and proceed forthwith to the Lost Valley, to the Vegetable Garden, or to the path that needed laying urgently, and the job would be blitzed at a stroke.

Certainly there were volunteers involved in the project, but apart from groups from the British Trust for Conservation Volunteers who came for a fortnight here and there, and regulars such as Dave Burns, who is now in charge of car parking, the work was carried out entirely by the gardening staff. It has long been a tradition amongst the staff to trade interesting comments and queries from visitors. At the end of a long day's digging, as the tools were being washed at the stone trough in the Melon Yard, and the mud was being scraped from boots and oilskins, the question that rankled most was: 'Are you volunteers?'

The reason it inspired feelings of indignation was simple: we felt so privileged to have been given the chance to restore such an extraordinary garden. We felt, too, the constant presence of those who had created what we were trying to restore, such that, in some curious way, each of us felt the need to justify our own presence there. The very least we could do was to give our absolute all. And that was what we felt we were doing; we were all tremendously proud of our efforts. It was as though we were desperate not to let our predecessors down, knowing what high standards they had set and, judging by the fertility of the soil and the complexity of the glasshouses and infrastructure, the fantastic results they had achieved.

Today that insecurity that we felt, as the poor relations of great gardeners – coupled with the added worry that we never knew from one day to the next whether the project could maintain the rate at which it was moving – has disappeared; the lease from the Tremayne Estate has twenty-one years left to run, with the option to renew after that. There is now 'whole site security' as never before.

Peter Stafford, the managing director, has made it his priority to turn a fragile and precious garden, dependent entirely upon visitors for its survival, into a successful business. With a core of 100 staff, peaking at 135 in the busy summer months, and a business which is still expanding in its complexity and therefore still proving as costly as ever, this is no mean feat.

Whilst always claiming to have no knowledge of gardening, Peter cites three key issues for the continuing success of Heligan as what must inevitably be called, in today's terms, a visitor attraction and therefore a product. The first is the food grown in the productive gardens, the 'jewel in the crown', as he calls them. The second is the way in which we manage the land, and the third pertains to the approach we take to the wildlife on the estate. These three factors, combined with the visitor experience, are at the core of Heligan's success. Combining the best of the old with the best of the new allows both visitor and staff to re-establish a connection with the soil – soil that was sweated over by whole generations before us.

But undoubtedly Heligan might still remain in the grip of tangled briers today if the right people had not been in the right place at the right time. From the early days of the restoration it has been a story of individuals and charismatic leaders. Philip has always been fond of illustrating this point by quoting Cassius in *Julius Caesar*, as he tried to persuade Brutus to join the conspirators: 'Why, man, he doth bestride the narrow world like a Colossus; and we petty men walk under his huge legs and peep about to find ourselves dishonourable graves.' Whether obtaining money, digging the garden or accumulating people and ideas, someone always stepped forward to be that colossus; but the biggest of all, who put us all together and without whom the project would never have happened, was Tim Smit. And so the story goes on, looking and finding, uncovering the secrets of a great garden which stood on the brink of disappearing once and for all until, finally, it had waited long enough and its time came again.

FOLLOWING PAGE
*A rainbow colours up a ripening field of fodder maize at the top of Pentewan Hill. The tree line in the foreground is a deep valley, typical of the type found along the Cornish coast.*

# Index

# Acknowledgments

The idea for this book was entirely due to Melanie, who said: 'If I am going to move to Cornwall I will need a project.' And whilst I, with my insider knowledge, tried at first to point Melanie this way and that and presumed I could tell her things that would make her leap out of bed, pre-dawn, and rush to the gardens to photograph, she connected with the spirit of Heligan and did it in the way that only she can. The results are wonderful. Forty thousand words and hundreds of pictures later, it has been some project.

But this book would never have got off the ground without the wholehearted encouragement and support of Candy Smit and Peter Stafford, the managing director. Candy was committed to the project from day one, and such is her love and passion for Heligan that she helped to ensure that the glory of the garden was brought to the fore. She gave boundlessly of her deep knowledge of the innermost wonders of the place, and was unrelenting in her enthusiasm.

To me it feels like completion. For, despite spending several years away from Heligan and out of Cornwall altogether during the last few years of the 1990s, a large part of me never left at all. That is the glory of the county and the specific character of Heligan. Like the rain on the west wind, they are inextricably linked and mildly addictive. To have the chance to write about a garden that I spent so much time in during the early years of restoration, and again in recent years, has been an absolute pleasure – and for that I must thank Weidenfeld & Nicolson for commissioning the book.

The collection of photograph albums that is now in my father's possession reach from far back in the nineteenth century up to the present day. When I first began working at Heligan in 1993 I remember looking in the index for references to the garden and finding several. They never came to light then because they didn't bring any remarkable insights to the layout of the garden or have much specific relevance to the restoration. But the fact that my grandfather convalesced at Heligan after Gallipoli could not be more relevant. My grandmother, who took the pictures used in this book, died when I was a small boy, my grandfather soon after the Second World War; and without them my Heligan story would be much the poorer. So thanks, Dad, for letting me paw the 1915–17 book into submission.

Everyone at Heligan has offered their unfailing support through the last eighteen months, from Tim Smit, who hired me, and who kindly wrote the foreword, all the way through to Charles Fleming. Charles was the very first person I saw on the day I began work at Heligan in October 1993, and he has published countless books on the gardens himself. No one was more thrilled than Charles when I told him that Melanie and I were producing a book, and no one could have given more encouragement. Every week he would look up from the patch of ground he was weeding, hoof pick in hand, and ask, 'How's the book coming on?' Sometimes I would squirm in agony, other times I would pull his leg and tell him, 'Be ready next week Chas,' but always I felt supported. So finally it is ready Chas; thank you for keeping me up to my work.

All the gardening and estate staff have, as always, been wonderful. So much pride is taken in the work that is carried out at Heligan, in all departments, and it really does show through in Melanie's photographs. Thank you Kathy for your beautiful labels, and thank you Sylvia for allowing Clive to be so generous with that pineapple!

As the text reached completion, I have to admit that I felt a little nervous when Tim and Candy both asked to read it. They could not have been more sympathetic, and they put my mind at rest. Philip McMillan Browse, with whom I have worked closely over the years, was kind enough to read it too, and put one or two horticultural matters to rights. He also kindly checked the captions, so thank you all for making yourselves available with your valuable knowledge and support.

It has been a joy working with the team at Weidenfeld & Nicolson. As the first block of text reached Michael Dover, my heart was in my mouth, but the reply came back simply to keep it coming; a response I could never have dreamed of, and one that put me at rest and allowed me to carry on and relax into the job. It was just what I needed, because writing about Heligan is a dream, so thank you Michael for giving me my head. We have had many laughs along the way with Michael and David Rowley, the genius art director who has been fantastic throughout, including a scene where the background noise of waves lapping on the shore on a sweltering July afternoon had to be converted to central London traffic roar for the benefit of the person on the other end of the mobile telephone.

Clive Hayball was in the Weidenfeld offices on our very first trip there in the autumn of 2002, and we knew at once he was the man for us. He has designed the book beautifully, with skill and sensitivity, and we are grateful for all your help Clive, it looks fantastic.

As far as editing is concerned, Michael has been gentle with me over some appalling slang, woeful grammar and questionable punctuation, and the whole text has been finally sorted out by the wonderful Jennie Condell, who has had to decipher some terrible horticultural and provincial nonsense. Thank you both for your patience and understanding.

And lastly, to our agent Jane Turnbull, who put us together with Weidenfeld & Nicolson, a huge thank you for getting the whole thing going. It has been the best of fun and we have enjoyed every minute of it.

Much has been written about Heligan over the last twelve years, and a mass of photographs has been taken charting the progress of the restoration. To have been part of all the tremendous achievements over that time is a great privilege. I have always felt the eyes of the old gardeners watching us with interest through the seasons, hopefully approving of our successes and no doubt chuckling at our failures; such is the life and history of the place. Having completed the book, we both feel indebted to Heligan for allowing us to delve so deeply into the gardens, and I am indebted to Melanie, for portraying so much, so beautifully.

First published in the United Kingdom in 2004 by Weidenfeld & Nicolson, a division of the Orion Publishing Group

Text copyright © Tom Petherick 2004
Pictures copyright © Melanie Eclare 2004

Except p. 13, bottom right; p. 17, top right; p. 107, top right all © Herbie Knott. Pages 176-7 all © eco-watch. All black and white photographs taken from the Petherick family photograph albums.

Design and layout copyright © Weidenfeld & Nicolson

Printed and bound in Italy by Printers SRL and LEGO

A CIP catalogue record for this book is available from the British Library.

Design director: David Rowley
Designed by Clive Hayball
Edited by Jennifer Condell

ISBN 0 297 84344 3

Weidenfeld & Nicolson

The Orion Publishing Group
Wellington House
125 Strand
London WC2R 0BB

ABOVE *What garden would be complete without robins and snowdrops in spring?*
PAGE 2 *From the top of the Jungle, the boardwalk begins to meander its way into the far reaches of Heligan's extraordinary valley garden. The gnarled red trunks of* Rhododendron arboreum *line the route by the top pond, promising an exotic route into the past.*
PAGE 3 *Two young ones pause at the bottom of the Jungle, to catch their breath and their reflections in the water.*
PAGE 4 *So many plants were found in the same condition as this* Rhododendron arboreum, *sprawling and helpless, as old age caught up and nobody was there to rescue them.*
PAGE 5, LEFT Pulsatilla vulgaris. RIGHT *The gardener's friend. (Robin!)*

Heligan Gardens are open every day except Christmas Eve and Christmas Day from 10 a.m.